An Intelligent Approach To Buying Real Estate

George A. Cave

Cave Publishing
Newbury Park, California 91320

Copyright © 1997
by
George A. Cave

All rights reserved.
No part of this book may be reproduced
in any form or by any means,
except for advertising
without written permission.

This book is designed to provide accurate and authoritative information in regard to the subject matter covered. It is sold with the understanding that the author and publisher are not engaged in rendering legal or accounting services. If legal advice or other expert assistance is required, the services of a competent professional person should be sought.

All right reserved. This book or any part thereof may not be reproduced in any form whatsoever, whether by graphic, visual, electronic, filming, microfilming, tape recording or any other means, without the prior written permission of the author.

Cave Publishing
PO Box 282, Newbury Park, California, 91319
(800) 341-0914

An Intelligent Approach To Buying Real Estate

Forward

This book was written with the idea that every person in this country should be able to own a home of their own. When you have read this book completely it will become apparent that anyone who wishes to own one house, ten houses, one hundred houses or more, will be able to do so using your ingenuity instead of your hard earned money.

The information contained in this book does not require any special knowledge or skills to perform, just a willingness to get off of the sofa and do it.

This book shows ways to buy property with "no money down", to all cash purchases. It shows that even if a person has no job, no money, and no credit, they can still purchase property. This book shows how a person who filled bankruptcy only two years ago can purchase a home with a loan guaranteed by the United States government with only a 3% down payment for a loan up to $155,250. This book also shows how to get a loan guaranteed by the United States government for up to $25,000 to fix-up your property, even if you have no equity at all in your home.

I was motivated to start investing in real estate by a job I hated and a supervisor I despised. In my first year of real estate investing I purchased 17 houses. Every time my boss would irritate me I would go out and purchase another house.

This book also informs the reader that real estate investing has many benefits but it also has it's drawbacks as well and gives instruction on the proper way to invest and to maintain those investments. Why learn the hard way when you can take advantage of the experience of seasoned investors. This book takes the reader through actual purchases, pointing out the benefits and the mistakes that were made and how to avoid them.

Whether your looking to purchase a home for yourself or for investments. If you are already investing in real estate and wish to further your knowledge and possibly pick up something new, this book is a must read.

CONTENTS

Chapter One: Why Real Estate   5

Chapter Two: What to Buy   18

Chapter Three: Financing   30

Chapter Four: Buying A House   46

Chapter Five: Buying Foreclosures   58

Chapter Six: Creative Buying   68

Chapter Seven: Tenants   85

Chapter Eight: Real Estate And The IRS   94

Glossary of Terms, Examples and insights   110

Amortization Schedules   180

Index   185

Chapter One

WHY REAL ESTATE

I am going to assume that, since you bought this book, you already have a fairly good idea of the benefits of owning real estate and I don't intend to spend a great deal of time trying to convince anyone that real estate is a good investment. Anyone with any amount of knowledge of the accumulation of wealth already knows that the majority of millionaires in this country made their money in real estate and even those who made it in some other fashion own a substantial amount of real estate as an investment.

Real estate has had an average appreciation in price of 10% a year for the last 50 years. That's an excellent rate of return on an investment that someone else is going to pay off for you, specifically, your tenants. Real estate is one of the

An Intelligent Approach To Buying Real Estate

only investments where you can leverage large amounts of assets without putting up very much money. For instance, anyone could go out tomorrow, put 20% down on a home and if they are creditworthy, could purchase that house by financing the balance. Name one other investment that you can do that with, and not only that, but in the case of rental property, the tenants will be paying off the mortgage for you. If you can acquire the property with little or no money out of your pocket, that makes the return on your investment unbeatable.

"Buying Properties Is The Easiest Part Of Real Estate Investing"

There's also a great deal of security in owning real estate. No matter what else happens in this country, people are going to have to live somewhere. What this book tries to accomplish is to make you successful in your real estate buying, regardless of whether it's a home for your own personal use or as an investment. This book will also attempt to give you enough information to avoid all of the pitfalls that can occur in real estate investing. Yes, it's true that more millionaires have been made in this country by investing in real estate than by any other means, but there's probably a greater number of people that have gone bankrupt as well. We want to be the former. Maybe we won't all be millionaires but at least you'll have the knowledge to make logical, intelligent real estate transactions.

I also am not going to spend a great deal of time going over the mechanics of buying real estate. I had read every book there was before I went out and started to buy properties and couldn't remember any of the technical terms or procedures. There is a glossary in the back of the book that will help you understand the terms and technicalities of real estate investing. Unlike most glossaries, it also gives examples and in-depth insight to many of the terms. For instance, if you were to look up the term 'estate planning', it would not just give a text book definition but examples and helpful hints. If you have a question about insurance, you will see that in addition to a definition it explains the various types of insurance and which ones I recommend. Remember as you read these comments and recommendations that they are just that - mine. If doing something a certain way is working for you, by all means keep doing it that way.

"Like Other Professionals, Realtors Are Not All Created Equal"

The first question that we have to get out of the way is: Why anyone would want to purchase real estate? The magnitude of benefits are obvious with just a few of them being previously stated, but a more pressing question is what are you going to do with it once you acquire it. Why are you buying it? What is its purpose? Are you going to live in it, rent it out or turn it around for a quick profit?

I found out right away in my real estate buying experiences that acquiring property was the easy part. On my first day of real estate investing I bought three units, a house and a duplex, with 'no money down'. It was what came next that took more thought and effort.

An Intelligent Approach To Buying Real Estate

Some people want to buy a house to raise a family in and have the security of owning their own home. Some people might want to have a source of retirement income while for others it may be a full time occupation. For whatever reason you wish to invest in real estate, this book should be able to answer most of your questions, or at least send you to a place where they will get answered. You don't need to be a Realtor or possess any special knowledge to invest successfully in real estate. You can invest with the help of a Realtor or without one. If you wish to use a Realtor, search out the best ones and use them. The easiest way to determine who are the best Realtors is to ask about their listing and sales success, or simply ask for the Realtor who sells the most property. Like all other types of professionals, Realtors are not all created equal. You would probably not take your car to just any mechanic, nor a toothache to just any dentist. Take your time and find a Realtor that suits your needs. The right Realtor can help you accumulate a great deal of real estate very quickly.

As you get started in investing you may find it easier to use a Realtor until you feel more comfortable. I bought my first few houses using a Realtor and was glad I did. We will see that a good Realtor can do a lot of work for you giving you more time to focus on other things if you should decide to continue to use their services.

One very important thing to remember when using a Realtor is to make sure that he or she does what YOU want him to. You can better decide for yourself what is best for you. There are some Realtors that were lured to the real estate business because of the unlimited income potential but have not followed it up with the proper education. You will find that these types of "get rich quick" Realtors don't last long in hard times. So pick a seasoned veteran with a good selling history.

A friend of mine recently wanted to buy a house for himself and his sister as their primary residence. (Why not, how many people are fed up with making someone else wealthy by paying off their mortgage for them?) He had been out with some Realtors and came to the belief that he could not afford to buy a house in our area. Everything he looked at was to high in price and he was being told that he needed to come up with 20% of the purchase price as a down payment. I sat down with him for only an hour and explained to him the truth about buying real estate. Whether it's for your own personal residence or for an investment, it's the same. He went out and bought a beautiful two story home with only a 5% down payment, and at a price and a payment that he could afford, but not before going through several Realtors. Realtors, like most other professionals are not all created equal. Take your time and find one who suits your needs. So whatever your objective is, it would be best for you to read this entire book. It should be able to help you to realize your dreams.

The reason that I got started investing in real estate was, in a word, my boss. I was in a job that I couldn't stand, working for a man that I despised. Maybe you know someone in this same situation. I knew that if I worked as hard at my own business as I did at this job I would have to be successful.

I had recently bought a home in Newbury Park, California with my G. I. Bill. That's a Veterans Administration loan (VA loan). These loans are guaranteed by the US government in the event of default and there's no money down required. This is one of the easiest ways to buy a house. The loan is the

An Intelligent Approach To Buying Real Estate

easiest to qualify for and if you do it right you won't even have to pay closing costs. (Most of the terms will be explained throughout the book, but if you just can't wait, go ahead and use the glossary.)

In my case, I didn't know anything about buying a house and I was at the mercy of the Realtor. It worked out alright in the end in that it only cost me $1,500 out of my pocket to purchase a $73,500 home. But if I knew then what I know now I probably would have put that $1,500 in my pocket instead of paying it. Read on.

Going to work every day was drudgery and there was no relief in sight. My financial condition came to depend on the sixteen hours a week overtime I was working and I was afraid that if I changed jobs that I would not be able to bring home the same amount of money. How on earth was I ever going to get away from this boss I couldn't stand and live the life that I wanted for myself and my family?

Then I read an ad in the newspaper that a real estate guru was speaking in Los Angeles and it was absolutely free. The speaker had written several books on buying real estate and was known to be quite the specialist in amassing a fortune in property with "no money down".

I went to the lecture and while I was there I signed up for a two day real estate seminar on the following weekend. This was in the early 1980's and the course cost me $500. (This book cost considerably less and you will get more out of it.) I also bought every book that was available at the seminar, another $400. There were 500 people at the seminar and at its end the instructor opened it up for questions. Inevitably, one of the people asked that if it were so easy to make a fortune in real estate, why was he selling the information for a mere $500?

He answered by explaining that out of the 500 people that were in the room, only five of us would do anything with the information, and even if we all went out and starting buying houses today, the real estate pie was big enough for us all. I was determined to be one of the five people that he was talking about and immediately went home and read every book, cover to cover.

I had spent several years in Phoenix while I was stationed in the Air Force and felt that the real estate market in Phoenix was primed for what I wanted to do. The homes in the area of California where I lived were very high priced, but the rents were not. A three bedroom, two bath home cost $150,000 and the rent was only $1,000 a month. That would have created a real big negative cash flow. (Negative cash flow-meaning that it costs more to pay the mortgage and expenses than the rent being collected.) In Phoenix however, I could buy a house for $50,000 and the rent would be $500, or a better than break-even cash flow.

"Real Estate Is A Living, Breathing Organism"

I knew that if I waited until I was completely ready to start buying houses, I never would. So after one month of reading and studying the material I had bought at the seminar, I drove out to Phoenix. I got a hotel room and a newspaper and I went over the properties in the newspaper that looked good to me and started making phone calls the next morning. (My criteria for finding possible purchases was to find listings that

An Intelligent Approach To Buying Real Estate

said the owner was willing to carry a second trust deed and that the first mortgage was less than 50% of the value of the home. We will see why this was important for this type of purchase.) I probably made every mistake there was to make, but by the end of the day I had purchased three units, a house and a duplex, all without any money down and all of them having a positive cash flow. At that I drove back home.

If this story doesn't excite you, nothing about real estate will. The reason is that by the time you're done reading this book you will know more than I did when I went out and bought those first properties. But before we get too far ahead of ourselves, let's get down to some basics. The last thing I would want to do is to give you just enough information to be dangerous and have you go out and start buying properties before you know what you're going to do with them.

As I said earlier, buying houses was the easiest part of real estate investing. What to do with them once you have them is the real question. It would be foolish to arbitrarily go out and buy a bunch of houses for no other reason than the fact that you can. I know this because that's exactly what I did. I acquired seven homes before I started to ask myself these questions. The first question was "When is the money going to start pouring in"? A couple of negative cash flows and you could be in some serious trouble. Real estate investing should not be a constant burden on your checkbook. Each property should be self sufficient, it should take care of itself financially, of course. The income that a particular piece of property generates should be more than enough to pay the mortgage, taxes, insurance, maintenance, vacancy and additional income taxes, if necessary. As we will see, the income tax advantage of owning real estate is excellent. You can make money on the property every year but still take a loss on your tax return. (Is this a great country or what?) Show me one other investment like that.

The first thing to remember about real estate is that it is a living, breathing organism. If you feed it, nurture it, and maintain it, it will reward you for the rest of its life. If you ignore it, take from it without giving back, it will make your life miserable. This is the area that most people don't think through before investing. Or they seem to think that someone else will take care of it for them. WRONG!

There are many types of investments available today and real estate is only one of them. If you are not prepared to spend the time and energy, and sometimes your money, to do this properly, it might be best to think about investing in something else. Real estate will continue to reward you if you do what is required of you. How many other investments can you think of that someone else will effectively buy for you? I can't think of any. In real estate, you can buy a house for no money out of your pocket, take a loan out on the entire purchase (we'll talk more about this later) and have someone who lives in the house pay you rent, which will eventually pay off the entire loan amount and then you are sitting there still collecting the rent on a piece of property that's yours free and clear. **This is the ultimate retirement account.** (Buy one property a year for ten years, pay them off on a 15 year amortization schedule and in 25 years, or sooner, they will all be paid in full and you collect all of the rent as your retirement income.)

An Intelligent Approach To Buying Real Estate

There are other types of investments that I also have and I would definitely recommend that real estate not be your only nest egg. For Example, I put 10% of all of my income, including rent, into a high yield mutual fund. These funds have gotten as high as a 72% annual return. That is rare, but over the long run an average rate of return of 15 percent is very conservative. If a person puts just $2,000 a year into a high yield mutual fund that averages just 15% a year, in 20 years they will have $237,670 and in thirty years, over one million dollars.

By increasing this yearly contribution just a little, the end result is amazing. So few people understand the real power of compound interest. See table 1.1 for an example of the effects of a $2,000 per year investment. If you invest $4,000 then double the results, if you invest half, then the result would be halved. I have a program on my computer that will calculate any scenario imaginable. This same program can calculate loan payments as well.

A lot of companies have a savings plan for their employees that they contribute to as well. This is an excellent way to increase your pay without getting a raise. When the company I was working for instituted these types of plans, my monthly pay was increased by $150 per month just because of the money that the company was contributing to my accounts.

There was a time when I would spend hours a week tracking stocks and doing the investing myself but I could never outperform mutual funds. In Peter Lynch's book, "One Up On Wall Street", he writes about school children that

George A. Cave

Table of deposits of $2,000 per year at a 15% rate of interest

# of Yrs	Deposit	Total	# of Yrs	Deposit	Total
0	-	2,000.00	20	2,000.00	237,620.24
1	2,000.00	4,300.00	21	2,000.00	275,263.28
2	2,000.00	6945.00	22	2,000.00	318,552.77
3	2,000.00	9986.75	23	2,000.00	368,335.68
4	2,000.00	13,484.76	24	2,000.00	425,586.03
5	2,000.00	17,507.48	25	2,000.00	491,423.94
6	2,000.00	22,133.60	26	2,000.00	567,137.53
7	2,000.00	27,453.64	27	2,000.00	654,208.16
8	2,000.00	33,571.68	28	2,000.00	754,339.39
9	2,000.00	40,607.44	29	2,000.00	869,490.29
10	2,000.00	48,698.55	30	2,000.00	1,001,913.84
11	2,000.00	58,003.33	31	2,000.00	1,154,200.91
12	2,000.00	68,703.83	32	2,000.00	1,329,331.05
13	2,000.00	81,009.41	33	2,000.00	1,530,730.71
14	2,000.00	95,160.82	34	2,000.00	1,762,340.31
15	2,000.00	111,434.94	35	2,000.00	2,028,691.36
16	2,000.00	130,150.19	36	2,000.00	2,334,995.06
17	2,000.00	151,672.71	37	2,000.00	2,687,244.32
18	2,000.00	176,423.62	38	2,000.00	3,092,330.97
19	2,000.00	204,887.17	39	2,000.00	3,558,180.62

Table 1.1

An Intelligent Approach To Buying Real Estate

fictitiously invested in stocks, tracked them and made a very good return.

The reason for this good return was that children picked companies that they liked. They wore Nike tennis shoes, they bought Nike stock. It is a safe bet that if children like a product, the company that sells it will do very well. Lynch goes on to say that the normal person can select profitable stocks as well as the professional stock broker or mutual fund manager and gives many examples and strategies on how to do so.

After a while of selecting stocks for myself I found that I was spending so much time researching companies and tracking the stock market that I didn't have time to do the things that I wanted to do. So I gave the entire job over to a very competent financial advisor. He makes all of my mutual fund investments for me and his services don't cost me a dime. Great, now I can spend more time on my real estate and having fun. The whole point of this is to not invest everything in any specific area. Real estate is only one part of a well balanced and diverse investment portfolio. I buy as much real estate as I want. Why? Because it costs me almost nothing out of my pocket to acquire and as long as each property pays for itself and I put 10% of the rent into a high yield mutual fund, I'm happy. Many of you may not be able to do both right away: invest in real estate and put away 10%-but it certainly is something to strive for.

For me, I truly enjoy buying houses and I also enjoy working on them. The only thing I don't like about rental properties is having to deal with the tenants. This is the one drawback in rental property. Someone has to rent it. This would be a good time to decide if you are in for the long haul or the quick bucks. There's something to be said for both plans. I have done both and prefer the long haul because the longer you own a property the more it will give you. However, many people have made a fortune buying a property and then turning right around and selling it. This is especially true in distressed properties. If you can buy a house for fifty cents on the dollar, put in a little fix-up and turn around and sell it at full value, by all means do so. My point is for you to know what you intend to do with the property BEFORE you buy it. Fix-up properties take more out of pocket money but are very often worth it. Whether it's a 'no money down' deal or an all cash transaction the process is the same. We will be going over all of this in more detail later on. Again the point of this is that you should know what you intend to do with the property BEFORE you buy it.

Chapter Two

WHAT TO BUY

Now that you've made the decision to buy a house, it's time to decide what house to buy. I'm going to start right off with the first rule of picking a house. "Never fall in love with real estate before you own it." If you do you will make some of the most ridiculous decisions of your life. Remember, until you own it, it's just a house. So it's important to know what it is you are looking for before you begin. Most of the time I won't even go to see a property until I know that the seller and I can make the deal. What good is it to spend all your time looking at homes that you're not going to buy? Most of my negotiating is done over the phone and only if it sounds like we'll be able to negotiate an equitable arrangement do I bother to preview the property.

That's not to say that I go into every detail about the transaction over the phone. I just want to know what the sellers mortgage ratio is and if he's willing to carry a note on the property. The rest we can discuss after I see the property and talk to the owner. It works the same if you are going to use a Realtor. I ask him the same questions with the answer very often being, "It never hurts to ask." So true. Most of the time the listing agent knows the mortgage ratio and whether or not the owner is willing to carry a note. It isn't until we actually sit down and write out the purchase contract that we start talking about who's going to pay the closing costs and fees and details of the note that he's going to carry. (Sometimes the owner may ask for a little higher price if he has to pay all of the costs, but that's alright with me as long as my out of pocket expenses are minimized.)

"Never Fall In Love With Real Estate Before You Own It."

(In this book, we're not going to be going over the myriad of forms that are used in real estate. That could be a book in itself. Each State, even though they usually do the exact same thing, may have subtle differences in their forms. In California, you can call the California Association of Realtors for a copy of their book of real estate forms. This book has all of the forms used in real estate transactions in the state or California, and it only costs around $12. Their phone number is (213) 739-8227. Most states have a similar association, ask a Realtor for the phone number.)

An Intelligent Approach To Buying Real Estate

As I mentioned earlier I didn't need to have any knowledge of how to fill out the forms when I started to purchase homes and even now I have an escrow officer do it for me. You can do the exact same thing. If you're not using a Realtor and you can come to the basic terms with a seller, just call a local escrow company and tell them that you want to open an escrow and they will do the rest. An escrow company can do nothing without escrow instructions, which all start with the purchase contract, which they will write up for you. Remember, they are being paid for their services and whether you are buying one house or one house per month, they are very helpful.

If you're looking for a house either to live in or for an investment, the first thing to figure out is the price range or the maximum amount of monthly payment that you can afford. (As we go through the book you will see that there are ways to buy property that can get you a much nicer home for the same monthly payment as a smaller, less expensive one.) In the appendix there is a table that shows what the mortgage payment will be at a given percentage rate. This will give you the combined principal and interest amount, also called P&I. "Principal" is the amount of the payment that applies to the loan balance and "interest" is the amount of the payment that you are paying to the lender for loaning you the principal. However, there is more to a house payment than principal and interest. There are also taxes and insurance. I personally can't stand either of them. If you are an investor, both taxes and insurance are tax deductible as well as the interest on the mortgage. (Interest on rental property is business interest and is still tax deductible.) If it's your own home, the interest and taxes are deductible but not the insurance and principal.

The general rule for determining how much of a monthly payment you can afford is that is should be between 25 and 33 percent of your gross monthly salary. Most conventional loan companies will lend up to 33% if your total contractual obligations are no greater than 50%, including but not limited to car payments and credit cards,. For instance, if your gross pay is $4,000 a month, then your house payment could be between $1,000 (25%) and $1,320 (33%) per month. Your other contractual debts would then have to be no more than $680 (17%), figuring at the 50% total indebtedness rate. These figures vary significantly depending on many factors such as down payment, your credit history and whether or not the loan is a conventional loan or a government guaranteed loan such as an FHA or VA loan. Government guaranteed loans are usually much easier to qualify for. Rental properties are much more difficult to get new loans on with much higher down payments or equity required. We will be discussing "alternative financing" in detail later on.

"Before You Apply For Any Loans, Check Out Your Credit Report"

Your credit is very important when buying real estate but only if you intend to take out new or additional financing. Before you apply for any loans, check out your credit report. You will be amazed what's on it. It's very easy to do. Just look in the yellow pages of your local phone book under 'credit reporting' and there will probably be several agencies

An Intelligent Approach To Buying Real Estate

listed that will be able to supply you with a copy of your credit report. The fee is minimal, usually under $25, money well spent to see what it contains. If there are some things on your credit report that may not be positive, there are ways to get them cleaned up. Talk to the company that issued the report for details.

Sometimes your credit report will indeed have on it things that are not yours or things that you didn't know about. Before I bought my first home in California I had been living in Phoenix and had subscribed to the local newspaper. I moved back to California after my military service was complete and did not pay the final bill for that newspaper. The company couldn't find me and sent the bill to a collection agency and it was put on my credit report. I knew nothing about this and when I went to buy my first house, the lender refused to lend me the money until I paid the debt and sent them a letter explaining why it happened. It was not a big deal but it did slow down the process and it added one more thing I had to do to an already very hectic process that I still did not fully understand. So <u>before</u> you apply for any mortgages, check out your credit.

My criteria for buying houses when I first decided to invest was that it had to have a positive cash flow. This was due to the simple fact that I had no money. I also didn't want to buy homes that had a high payment in the event of a vacancy, remembering that if the tenant doesn't pay the rent, you still have to make the mortgage payment. Mortgage companies are funny about things like that!

I started to invest in real estate in the early 1980's and decided that I wanted to keep my homes under $50,000, (this turned out to be more of a guideline than a rule). These homes generally rented for $500 to $575 per month and the payment was generally less than $440 PITI (principle, interest, taxes and insurance). This would appear to have a positive cash flow of between $60 and $135 per month. Don't forget to add in the vacancy factor of 5% (of the monthly rent) and the maintenance factor of 7% (of the monthly rent) and of course any other expenses that you may have to pay such as utilities. If you have to pay any utilities the rent, of course, is higher but unless there's a really good reason to pay the utilities I don't. The only instances where I would have to pay utilities is in the case of some condominiums where the water, sewer and trash collection is a part of the homeowner's fees. (Don't forget to add in any homeowner fees, if applicable). This is not the case for all condominiums but it is something to think about when looking at condos to purchase. Again, my experience says not to pay the utilities unless you have to. You will be surprised how little conservation goes on when you are paying someone else's utilities. Another reason not to pay utilities is that it's just one more thing you have to keep track of and write checks for every month. It may not seem like much now, but wait until you own a couple of dozen homes. It's a major exercise just to write out the mortgage payments each month without having to write two or three more checks, per house, each month. On the one hand, mortgage payments stay the same month after month and so you could have checks printed automatically by computer or by your bank's autopay plan, if they have one. On the other hand, the amount paid for utilities change every month so they create quite a bit more of a check writing burden.

An Intelligent Approach To Buying Real Estate

There are many computer programs to help you keep track of expenditures and income but unless you have over 25 homes it is more trouble than it's worth. That is, unless you just have nothing better to do than to putz around on a computer. I, for one, don't have that kind of time.

So once you add in the vacancy and maintenance factor, which will be around $60 to $70 per month on a $50,000 house, your cash flow goes from break even to $65 per month. It might take a little while to get rich like this, but as we'll see later there are many ways to sweeten the pot. Remember, we've been talking about the payment and conventional 100% financing. There are ways to get much better deals and pay much less per month.

"Good Tenant's Are Worth Their Weight In Gold"

I found out very early in my investing ventures that houses with three bedrooms and two bathrooms rent out much better than do two bedroom units. This will also be true if you are looking to buy a house for yourself to live in, two bedroom homes are more difficult to sell than three bedroom homes and homes with two bathrooms are easier to sell than homes with only one bathroom. I also stay away from four bedroom rentals because a family that's big enough to require four bedrooms will inevitably have enough children to do considerable damage to the house. (Again, this is more of a guideline than a rule.)

Three bedroom houses seem to virtually never go vacant where the two bedroom units might go only three or four years

George A. Cave

before the tenants move out. Many times the tenant's family grows or their income rises and they want or need a bigger place. Most of the time they ask me if I have any three bedroom homes available. I usually don't because the three bedroom units stay rented for so long, but if I want to retain a good tenant, I tell them I will let them know the next time I have an opening or when I buy another one. That of course means that I will then have a vacant two bedroom but I would hate to lose a good tenant, and remember, good tenants are worth their weight in gold.

In the event a good tenant outgrows their house, I always ask them if they know someone that might want to rent the place that they're vacating. Personal referrals are probably the best source of good tenants. People don't generally recommend someone if they know them to be irresponsible. It makes them look bad. I also ask them why they are moving. Sometimes the answers are surprising. One tenant just wanted new carpet. She'd been renting from me for four years and I was going to replace the carpet anyway so I told her that I would replace it and she decided to stay. I also shop around for the best prices and best quality of replacements that I can find. If I have to replace a roof, I put on a 30 year roof that looks great. You'd be surprised how little more a high quality roof costs and it makes the house look so much better.

In the event of carpet replacement, I generally go to "D&K Hotel Liquidators" in Phoenix, or some similar discount carpet outlet. Hotel Liquidators sells the carpet that hotels have had replaced. If you can tell the difference between this carpet and new carpet you are doing better than I am and it lasts forever. Buying cheap carpet can turn into a full time job

An Intelligent Approach To Buying Real Estate

but buying carpet cheaply is a lifesaver, with carpet being one of the biggest recurring expenses. Once you replace a roof with a 30 year roof, you will probably never have another problem with it, but carpet is a completely different story. I've bought bargain carpet for $12 a yard installed and it's worn out in three to five years. This carpet from Hotel Liquidators costs about $6 a yard installed and never seems to wear out.

If D & K Hotel Liquidators don't have any carpet available when I need it, I then go to alternate sources. I don't know of any other city that has a hotel liquidator except for Phoenix. Look in the yellow pages under carpet and make a lot of phone calls, and go to see the carpet at several places before deciding what to buy. Sometimes you will be able to get a good deal on the carpet but then have someone else install it. No problem, again look in the phone book, under carpet installers or in your local newspaper, in the classified section. I stay away from national chain stores, it's easily twice the price for the same quality carpet at a discount carpet dealer.

Another big expense can be refrigerators and stoves if you are required to supply them. I don't unless it's a section 8 lease (government subsidized lease program, where the government pays up to all of the tenant's rent) and then it's required. I don't mess around with used appliances, I just pick out a basic model from Sears with no frills and it lasts for years. You might save a little bit of money up front by buying used appliances but over the long run they cost much more in repair costs and the continued replacement of them.

You also want to have a fairly good idea of the area of town you would like your house(s) to be in. If you are going

George A. Cave

to live in it, this may be of foremost importance. The same will hold true for your tenants. You want to be in a decent neighborhood, remembering that bad neighborhoods have a tendency to spread into good neighborhoods. So don't get too close to an area that's becoming run-down or crime ridden. (These tips are for the inexperienced buyer. As you gain in knowledge, wealth and courage you will probably find that buying in run-down areas is very profitable. Mainly because the current owners want out at any cost and if you know how to turn the area around a lot of money can be made and the neighborhood will really appreciate it. My experience shows that there are no more than a couple of bad tenants in a "bad neighborhood" and chances are the owner of the house they are living in wonders what's going wrong also. I have bought condos in a real tough part of town and become the president of the homeowners association board of directors and found that out of the 152 units in the complex, only about 6 of them, and their friends, were causing all of the problems. Once we threw them out it became a very nice place to live. It's also amazing that I have never felt that I was in any sort of danger even when evicting gang members. It's like there's some unwritten law about never messing with the landlord. Maybe it's because we're the only true authority these people ever see and they respect that. I have also never had to take one of these troublemakers to court. Once I send them a eviction notice, they move. The problem is they move into someone else's house. Be sure it's not one of yours. (Always screen your tenants thoroughly, credit reports are nowhere near as important as a call to their current landlord, and always ask if they would rent to them again.) If you are not prepared to

An Intelligent Approach To Buying Real Estate

take an active role in this type of an area, it's best to invest in an area that doesn't have these types of problems. Most areas do not have any problems like this but you want to be aware of the condition of the area that you are investing in.

"A Good Tax Strategy Will Improve Your Take Home Pay."

When you're looking for income property it is usually best to buy within 50 miles of your home. This makes repairs much easier, unless you plan to have someone else do them for you. If that's the case, don't plan on making much money. My experience shows that it's almost impossible to get a handyman to do anything for less than $100. It's much better if you can do the repairs yourself. I probably shouldn't be so cynical but repairs are a big part of whether you keep a positive cash flow or not. Many people have management companies that take care of everything for them. This is called passive investing. I don't recommend it, but it is a way to invest and not be bothered with the burden of tenants or maintenance. The IRS also takes a dim view on passive investors and limits the allowable tax deductions considerably. Always consult a tax specialist before buying your first property. A good tax strategy will help your take home pay more than most people could imagine.

I also don't like to buy houses on busy streets, because three bedroom homes will generally have children living in them and I wouldn't want my children to live on a busy street. Also you might want to make sure that there are schools and shopping within walking distance. This is very important if your plan is to rent to section 8 tenants. Very often they don't have a car. Then again sometimes their car is nicer than mine- go figure?

I have also found that houses that are hard to find always seem to be in nice, quiet neighborhoods. It seems that the troublemakers have difficulty finding houses that aren't on, or right off of, main streets. There are times when I have thought that graffiti wasn't so much a gang's way of marking their territory as much as it was writing down directions. (Graffiti is a big indicator of an area that you may want to stay away from investing in.)

Regardless whether you are buying a home to live in or to rent out, it's best to be very patient and selective in the location.

Chapter Three

FINANCING

Real estate investing is all financing. If you could get the proper financing you could buy the Taj Mahal. So the more you know about financing the better off you will be. If you're looking to buy a house for yourself it becomes very simple. When I buy properties for my own use or as an investment, I like to put as little down as possible.

It is true that the more money that one puts down on a property, the lower the monthly payment will be. But even if the payment is lower, you'll find you could probably make a better percentage rate in a decent mutual fund. Whatever the mortgage rate is, a better yield will come from a mutual fund and it's best to invest it there, or use it to buy more real estate. In addition, the amount of down payment required to make a meaningful reduction to the monthly payment would have to be substantial. For instance, if your mortgage is at 8%, the monthly payment savings would only be $7.34 a month for every thousand dollars that was put down. So it's easy to see that if a person was to put $5,000 down, the monthly payment would only be decreased by $36.70 per month. Now, if that same $5,000 was put into a long term high yield mutual fund, and you left it there for the same length of time as the mortgage on your house, 30 years in most cases, you would have $331,058 (at an average rate of return of 15%). The savings in interest from the loan, if you put the $5,000 down, would only be $8,208. I would prefer to put my cash into other investments. So for a $36.70 higher monthly payment you would make over $300,000. This is what makes real estate such an exciting investment, you can leverage high values of properties with little or no money, the tenants pay off the loan in the form of monthly rent and when it's all over you own the house with no mortgage and still collect the rents. And if you do it right, you'll be making money every month from your positive cash flow and be getting some very nice tax breaks.

When looking for financing, the first thing I do is pick up a "Lender's Report", sometimes called a "Lenders Survey". This is a chart of nearly all the lenders in the area, big and small, what their rates are, maximum loan amounts, percentage of down payments required, whether they do FHA and VA loans, length of loans and an assortment of other information. It's a good way to get a great deal of information quickly. Most real estate offices that I know of have these available at no cost. If you can't find a real estate office that carries them try a title company. Look them up in the yellow pages under "Title Companies". In California I generally just call "Continental

An Intelligent Approach To Buying Real Estate

Lawyers Title" over the phone and ask them to FAX me a copy without even leaving the house.

You'll see that there are all types of loans with various types of repayment plans. Conventional financing (without a government guarantee), FHA, and VA financing all offer similar programs. The **Fixed Rate Loan** is just as the name implies, it starts out at a specific interest rate and stays there for the life of the loan. There are also **Graduated Payment Loans**. This is when the loan payment gets larger as the years goes by. In some cases the loan stays at a low interest rate for many years. But be careful with this type of loan, because you may be paying less than the monthly interest that is accumulating. Meaning that as time goes on your principal balance increases even though you are making payments every month. So read the fine print on these types of loans. Sometimes it's the only way people can afford to purchase a home if they don't know any better.

Another type of loan is the **Variable Interest Rate Loan,** also known as **Adjustable Rate Mortgage (ARM)**. This type of loan got a lot of people in trouble during the late 1970's and early 1980's. While Jimmy Carter was President the interest rates skyrocketed and variable rate loans went right up with them. I personally feel that interest rates will never do that again. A Variable Interest Rate loan starts at an interest rate that is usually lower than a fixed rate loan and after six months to a year the interest rate is adjusted. The rate that you're charged is fixed to an economic indicator, called an 'index', such as the prime rate or a certain districts fund rate (there are many different districts throughout the country and depending upon where you live the district fund rate may be slightly different, but not by much). They will assign a certain amount of percentage points over that rate and as the index changes, so does your rate of interest, by the same amount. The difference between the index and the interest rate that you will be paying is called "the spread". For example, if the prime rate is 3% and your loan is tied to it with a 5 point spread, your interest rate will be 8%. The lender will adjust your payment price accordingly.

Variable Interest Rate loans can be very advantageous but read the fine print on these to make sure that the interest rate will also go down almost as much as it can go up. Variable Interest Rate loans also have a "cap" that limits the interest rate to a maximum amount. Five percent is not unusual, so if your initial rate is 6%, the highest that it can ever go is 11%. That's a whopper of an increase but the chance of that happening is really very slim. You can also get a history of the fund that your loan is tied to before you decide from whom to borrow. Where I live, the most popular rates are the 11th district funds and the prime rate. Both of these rates, along with others, are published each week, along with their long term history graph, in the Los Angeles Times newspaper, Saturday edition, in the Business Section.

FHA Financing:

If money is tight, and it usually is, first time home buyers might be better off looking into a government guaranteed loan such as FHA or VA financing. The down payment in the case of the FHA is only 3% of the loan amount. At the time of this writing, the maxumum loan amount that the FHA will finance

An Intelligent Approach To Buying Real Estate

is $155,250. (This amount may vary depending upon what part of the country you live in.)

The FHA has many different types of loans available and they change the requirements from time to time. FHA loans can be fixed rate or variable rate, it's up to you. The above example is just one of the types of FHA loans. Contact your local FHA lender for more information. Loan requirements are also very liberal and FHA loans are one of the easiest types of loans to qualify for. The criteria for purchasing a home through the FHA being: two years in the same line of work, two years since the filing of a bankruptcy. Three years for any foreclosures of property that you own, reasonably good credit with no bills currently at collections, and an income-to-mortgage ratio that shows that you can afford the monthly payment. (This is extremely simplified but by these guidelines one can see that this criteria is much more lenient than a conventional loan would be.)

FHA loans are guaranteed by what is called 'mortgage insurance' or MIP. This is insurance for the lender in the event of a default, meaning the owner is not making the payments. In this case the government pays off the loan for you and then sells the house to the highest bidder. This mortgage insurance is what makes the FHA a multi-billion dollars per year money maker for the government.

The cost of this MIP is about two-and-one-half percent of the loan amount. This amount is added on to the loan and fully amortized over the life of the loan. In the event you were buying a $100,000 home, the down payment would be $3,000 leaving a loan balance of $97,000. The MIP would be $2,425, for a total mortgage amount of $99,425. If you sell the house before the loan is paid off you can request a refund of the unused MIP from the FHA.

There are also closing costs involved in an FHA loan, as with all others, usually two to three percent of the amount of the loan, but a lot of the time the seller will pay them for you. It never hurts to ask. I always ask the seller to pay all closing costs and fees when I'm buying a house and the buyer to pay them when I'm selling a house. They may very well say no but the worst that will happen is that you'll be asked to pay the standard, one half. Never forget that just because everybody else pays half of the costs doesn't mean that you have to, it's all negotiable.

If you think that an FHA loan may sound like what you're looking for then call up any of the FHA lenders on your Lenders Report and ask for detail on the various types of loans that the FHA has to offer. After a review of the many types of loans the FHA offers I cannot imagine anyone not being able to afford a home. In most cases the mortgage payment would be less than rent. But then if everybody owned their own home, I'd be out of business! Realtors will usually have information on FHA loans as well. You can also get pre-approved for a loan before you even start to look for a house. This way you will know the price range you'll be looking for. Having been pre-approved is a big plus in that the seller knows that you are serious and it takes away some of his anxiety knowing that you are already approved. The only thing that will now have to be approved is the house.

The FHA and the VA require inspections of the prospective property and they must meet their standards or the seller has to make the necessary repairs to bring it up to those

An Intelligent Approach To Buying Real Estate

standards. I always insist, when buying a home from a private person, that the home be in move-in condition. That means thoroughly cleaned, including the carpet, fresh paint, inside and out if necessary and an immaculate yard. Always check under the sinks for any signs of water leaks. And make sure the <u>seller</u> fixes them <u>before</u> you close escrow. A lot of times the water will be turned off, especially if the house is vacant, so initially look for signs of water damage and if at all possible have the seller turn on the water for a final inspection of the plumbing. Water will damage a house faster than anything except for a fire.

All sales should have an inspection by you prior to your signing the final documents. Do not take this inspection lightly.

In the case of buying a home through the FHA or VA you will probably be using a Realtor. Very often they will know less about real estate than you will. Don't let them do anything that you don't want them to do. I also find it best to go and talk to the seller with him when he presents the offer. This of course depends on your Realtor.

Remember that the Realtor represents the <u>seller</u>, after all, he's the one paying the commission. Even if he tells you that the owner won't sell at your price, go ask him anyway. The Realtor is, by law, required to get the best price and terms for the seller that he can. No one is looking out for your interests as a buyer except for you. The Realtor is also required, by law, to submit all offers to the seller for his consideration. (Again this is California law and it may be different in your state, but I doubt it.)

George A. Cave

There are buyer's agents, that is, someone that would be representing you in the purchase, but you, the buyer, are responsible for his fee. But then again that's also negotiable. If you should decide to use a buyer's agent, once you find a house to buy, stipulate in the purchase contract that the seller is to pay his fee out of the commission. He would have had to pay commission to the seller's agent for the sale of the house if you had used one anyway. In this case, as in all others, listing and selling broker have to agree on the terms with regards to how the commission is divided. They are usually very cooperative, especially in times when real estate is moving slowly. (The listing broker is the broker, or his agent, that listed the house for sale. The selling broker, or his agent, is the broker that sold the house. Very often it's the same broker. Brokers like to list and sell their own houses, they make more money that way. The commission is generally 7% (negotiable) with 50/50 split going to the broker and the agent. If there's another broker/agent involved in the transaction, it would then be divided four ways instead of two. The point is, in many cases the selling broker/agent is not the listing broker/agent. So in the case of you using a buyer's agent, the seller may still pay his fee from the commission that he will have to pay anyway. The only difference is that the seller and his broker know, because it must be disclosed, that your agent is working in your best interest.)

FHA loans are assumable, meaning that if you are buying a house that has an existing FHA loan, you can take over the payments of that loan with a simple assumption. The escrow company will know how to handle this. There is no qualifying to assume an FHA loan so it can make it much easier to buy a

An Intelligent Approach To Buying Real Estate

home if your credit is less than perfect. This would mean, however, that a cash down payment would probably be necessary. I have purchased many homes with an existing FHA loan for as little as $1,000 down and assumed the payments.

FHA Title I Home Improvement Loan:

This is one of my favorite loans in the whole world and I recommend that everybody go take one of these out today. It is an FHA loan, guaranteed by the government, that requires no equity. That's right, no equity. No appraisal is done, the interest rate is fixed for between five and twenty years. The length of the loan is up to you. The interest rate is dependent upon several factors, like your credit history, if the home that's having the improvements is your personal residence or a rental.

The qualifying is the same as for FHA loans except that it's all based on your credit and the ability to repay the loan. This loan is available for people who want to fix up their personal residence and for investors who wish to improve their rental properties. The money is supposed to be used to improve the property and the lender will want to see a statement of the work that needs to be done and an estimate of the cost to perform the work. I have done several of these and I write up the estimate myself and the estimated cost is based upon someone else doing the job. I ended up doing the work myself for significantly less than a contractor would charge and was able to keep the balance of the loan. They do send people out to the house and verify that the work was done and of course it must be.

George A. Cave

VA Financing:

If you spent some time in the United States military and were honorably discharged, one of the benefits is the Veterans Administration loan guarantee program. The government rewards those who gave up a portion of their lives to serve their country. In this instance, the reward is to guarantee a home loan with 100% financing. That's right, no money down. This will be the first no money down deal we'll talk about but there are many more to come. This 100% financing applies only to the purchase price and not to the associated costs of the purchase. It's generally safe to assume that your costs, if split the conventional way, is about three to four percent of the purchase price, so a $100,000 home would cost you three to four thousand dollars, out of pocket, to buy it. Again, ask the seller to pay all of these costs. You'll be surprised what a motivated seller will pay for.

The VA requires a 2% funding fee paid at the time of escrow. This may be able to be added onto the loan amount as in the case of the FHA. The VA would not commit to a policy in this area. This funding fee is reduced depending on whether or not the veteran puts any money down. A 5% down payment reduces the funding fee to 1.5% and a down payment of 10% reduces the funding fee to 1.25%. I would just as soon pay the 2% and make no down payment. Veterans who are using their entitlement for a second, or subsequent time, who

An Intelligent Approach To Buying Real Estate

do not make a down payment of at least 5%, are charged a funding fee of 3%.

If you wish to use your GI bill to buy a home, contact your local Veterans Administration. They're in the white pages of your local phone book under United States Government heading, Veterans Administration Department. You may need to make several calls before you get hold of the right person. At the time of this writing the national 800 telephone number for the Veterans Administration is 1-800-827-1000. They will send you information about VA loans by asking for <u>VA Pamphlet 26-4</u>(Guaranteed Home Loans for Veterans) and <u>VA Pamphlet 26-6</u> (To the Home-Buying Veteran), or you could go to their office and pick them up. You can also get this information over the internet, the address is WWW.VA.GOV. If you are on-line the address if VAONLINE.VA.GOV.

One thing you will need in order to get your "certificate of eligibility" from the VA is your DD form 214. If you have misplaced it the VA will help you to get a copy of it, but it's a lot easier if you have it. If you will recall, it's the form that they gave you as you were being discharged and they told you "Whatever you do, don't lose this form".

Like FHA loans, VA loans have a maximum loan value, $203,000 at the time of this writing. That doesn't mean you can't buy a more expensive home using your VA entitlement, but the VA will guarantee only up to their maximum amount. If your home is more expensive than the amount guaranteed by the VA, the lender will generally require you to put down 25% on the amount over $203,000. For instance, if you want to buy a $250,000 home and take advantage of your VA loan guarantee. You would put no money down on the first

George A. Cave

$203,000 and 25% on the remaining $47,000. That would make the down payment $11,750.

VA loans also have a requirement to pass an inspection on the house with all discrepancies being repaired by the <u>seller</u>. Again, it is best to be pre-approved for this type of loan because the government, in the case of the VA and the FHA, are rather slow. It's not unusual for loan approval for them to take two months or more, and that's after the lender does all of the paperwork which could easily take another month. It's easy to see why a lot of sellers would not be willing to wait for this process to take place.

It's best to use a lender that is authorized to do automatic processing of VA loans. They can approve and fund the loan without waiting for the VA to review your credit application and the appraisal. Using one of these lenders helps to move things along more quickly. Nearly every major lender that funds VA loans is an authorized lender. A quick glance down the 'Lender's Report', that you can pick up from your local Realtor or Title Company, will list many authorized VA lenders.

VA loans are also assumable, but only upon the approval of the Veterans Administration. The new buyer would have to fill out the same paperwork that a new loan would require. The only difference is that it can be assumed by a person who is not a veteran.

I keep using the term 'loan guarantee' because in the case of the VA and FHA, they don't actually lend any money, the money is loaned through a conventional source like a bank or savings and loan. The government guarantees payment of the loan in the event that you don't make the payments. In the

An Intelligent Approach To Buying Real Estate

case of VA loans, the entitlement is also reusable. Once you sell your house and the original VA loan is paid off you can go buy another house using your VA entitlement again. However, the loan must be paid in full. That wouldn't be unusual if someone buys your house and finances it by getting a new loan. Also, the property must transfer out of your name. Again, this happens automatically when you sell the house. There is one circumstance where this second requirement does not apply. For instance, you could use your VA entitlement to buy a house with no money down, refinance it when the equity is available, then use your VA again to buy another home with no money down you can still keep the original house. However, they will only allow you to do this only one time.

The reason for these rules, as I am fully aware, is that the VA doesn't want you to amass a great deal of property using your VA entitlement. However it is one way to do so. I bought my first house using my VA and after couple of years I refinanced it using a conventional loan and therefore satisfied the first requirement of reinstating my entitlement. The next thing I did was to transfer the property into the name of a very close friend, satisfying the second requirement. I got my entitlement back and then could use it again to buy another home with no down payment. I then transferred the original property back into my name. (There's no law against this, the VA even told me how to do it, but I must caution you, be very careful who you transfer title to your house to, for they do not have to give it back! I had him sign a deed back to me at the same time I transferred it out of my name and just didn't file it until my entitlement was reinstated.) But because of changes in their policies this would now only be necessary after you used your entitlement <u>twice</u> without selling the house secured by the guarantee. You could have as many other homes as you like, this only applies to homes that you plan to buy using your VA entitlement.

You can also refinance your VA loan without going through all of the hassles of new financing. This works out well in the event that interest rates drop. The VA will redo the guarantee, up to the original loan amount on the same house for the purpose of securing a lower interest rate. They will even finance any costs associated with the refinance as long as the amount doesn't exceed the original loan amount. Refinancing such as this can cost several points (percents) and sometimes in the case of a relatively new loan, the principal hasn't paid down that much and therefore you may have some out-of-pocket expenses but if the interest rate has decreased more than 1 1/2 percent, it's worth it. The difference in monthly payments is phenomenal. For example, the savings between a $100,000 loan at 9 percent compared to 7 1/2 percent is $105.41 per month. Over the term of the loan that amounts to a savings of over $37,000. Remember the power of compound interest works both ways.

Conventional Loans:

A conventional loan is what we have to get when the house is too expensive for an FHA or VA loan or they won't lend on the property, or for a variety of other reasons. The largest percentage of loans in this country are guaranteed by the government in some fashion. Buying income property may require a conventional loan as well. They usually require a

An Intelligent Approach To Buying Real Estate

significantly higher down payment, usually never less than 20%. There are always exceptions to this and we'll go over them in the next chapter.

There is no such thing as a 'normal' conventional loan, some will say that a 20% down payment with a 30 year pay back would be normal. Some companies will only require a 5% down payment, some will require significantly more than even 20%. This is when the Lender's Report comes in really handy.

Major newspapers usually have ads from companies with their rates and required down payment. The short of this is that the different types of conventional loans available are as numerous as different types of automobiles. Shop around and find the loan that best suits you, and don't feel as if a loan company or bank is doing you a favor by lending you money. The loan is secured by real estate and regardless of what else happens they are going to be make a fortune on this deal. The <u>interest</u> paid on a $100,000 loan paid back on schedule over 30 years financed at an interest rate of 8 percent is $164,000.

If you should get turned down for a loan, go to another lender or a different type of lender. A friend of mine got turned down to buy a home from one lender and one month later got approved by a different lender. This was for a conventional loan and if he had been turned down again he could have tried an FHA loan.

Conventional loans that are acquired with less than a 20% down payment are also required to pay mortgage insurance. The amount varies with the amount of down payment. In the event of a 5 percent down payment, the amount of mortgage insurance is about .0078 percent of the loan amount per month.

So in the case of a $100,000 loan after a 5 percent down payment the mortgage insurance payment would be $7.80 a month. This amount is added onto the mortgage payment and is made at the same time.

Owner Financing:

Here we go. Owner financing, or creative financing as it is often referred, is when you buy a property and the seller agrees to finance part or all of the transaction himself. He is acting as the lender. For instance, you're looking to buy a $50,000 home that already has a first mortgage of $25,000. This leaves a balance of $25,000 owed to the seller. You go out and secure a second trust mortgage for $12,500, which the seller will get at the close of escrow. This leaves $12,500 left that you still owe the seller and this will be carried by the owner in the form of a third trust deed. The terms on this remaining balance are completely up to the seller and the buyer.

For more information on owner carrybacks, read on.

Chapter Four

BUYING A HOUSE

    This chapter is dedicated to scenarios of actual house purchases that I have made. There are so many different ways to buy houses and depending on your situation and the sellers, you may have to be flexible to close the deal. I have found, as you probably will too, a particular strategy for buying that suits you best. This is called modeling. Once you find a model that suits you, you'll probably want to stick with it as long as it continues to satisfy your objectives.

    Some of the following stories are humorous, others are not, but all of them tell of many actual events that worked for me and will work for you as well. You will notice that I didn't posses any great amount of skill to work these deals and many times let others add the final touches. Don't feel that you have to know everything, (it even helps to play dumb when talking to sellers about buying their home) or do everything. Let those who have more experience than you help as much as possible. They are, after all, getting paid for their services.

After taking the seminar mentioned earlier, I set out to Phoenix with the intention of buying a couple of houses and see just whether or not this was going to work as easily as the books and lecturer claimed.

I planned to spend several days in Phoenix and after the seven hour drive checked into a motel. The next morning I got up and bought a newspaper and started to review the classified ads for houses to buy. I circled dozens of possibilities and without really having any kind of plan at all, started making phone calls. Picking up that phone was one of the hardest things that I ever had to do but after a few calls I felt very confident.

The reason it was hard to make the calls was that I was going to ask people to give me their house without giving them any money, or so I thought. (I had been led to believe that in a 'no money down' deal, that the seller wasn't going to get any money. I was very wrong.) I felt that there was no way anyone with any common sense whatsoever would do that. I was right. Without even knowing it I was about to find out how to make 'no money down' deals and get the seller what he needed out of the sale of his house. The theory is that if you can find a distressed seller, that is, one who needs to sell his property right away and is willing to give the buyer excellent terms, and satisfy his needs, then the rest is simple. (For examples of 'distressed seller' see the glossary)

The first house I became interested in was advertised in the newspaper as a 'no money down' deal. I called up the Realtor and he told me that the selling price was $62,000.

An Intelligent Approach To Buying Real Estate

(That was a little bit more expensive than I had planned but the rest of the terms worked out well.) This is one of those cases when you will be able to afford a more expensive home than you thought.

He went on to say that the seller had an FHA first mortgage of $27,000 and the plan was for me to take out a second mortgage for $20,000 and the owner would then carry a third mortgage for the balance of $15,000. This owner carryback would be without payments at an interest rate of 10%, all due and payable in five years.

A good practice to get into when the owner is carrying a note secured by a deed of trust is, in the note, put a clause that gives you, the buyer, the first right of refusal. That means that if the seller wishes to sell the note, he has to offer it to you first, with the same terms and conditions that his prospective buyer is offering. You don't have to do beat the prospective buyer's offer, just meet it.

These notes carried by the seller with no payments are almost worthless on the secondary mortgage market. (That's where people or institutions buy existing mortgages, usually at a discount. A $10,000 note might sell for $7,000 depending on the terms and conditions of the note. Maybe less, maybe more.) The reason is that there is no income on the note yet. When the note matures and payments are about to be made, or a balloon payment is about to become due, is when they start to acquire some value.

I met with the agent at the property and the house was in very good shape. The roof needed to be replaced so it was done during the escrow at the seller's expense. I agreed to the seller's terms and after signing the purchase contract I went

George A. Cave

down to the mortgage company to fill out the paperwork. (If I had to do it over again I would have asked, insisted, on a lower price, because I was the one qualifying for the second mortgage. The Realtor also told me that the seller was trying to sell it for the last six months with no takers. This is a perfect opportunity to take advantage of the situation.)

The mortgage company was Wells Fargo and they would finance up to 80% of the value of the house. In this case the owner was to carry a mortgage for the remaining 20% instead of me making a down payment. This is a little more of a risk for the mortgage company but then they were charging me 15% interest. The mortgage company still felt somewhat secure because if I didn't make the payments they would still be able to foreclose and if the seller didn't make up the payments and assume the balance of the loan they would be able to foreclose on the house, sell the property and still make money.

My monthly payments totaled $495 with the rent being $575, less expenses.

The next property I looked at, on the same day, was a duplex that had just recently been built. The owner owned it free and clear, meaning there were no mortgages on the property at all. He was asking $85,000 for the duplex and each of the units were renting out for $450 for a total rent of $900 per month.

This property was purchased the same as the previous house with the exception that instead of me qualifying for a second mortgage I was to qualify for a first mortgage in the amount of $60,000. The owner would then carry a second mortgage for the balance of $25,000. This owner carryback

An Intelligent Approach To Buying Real Estate

was to be at an interest rate of 10%, with no payments made until it was all due after three years. This made a payment of just under $545 PITI and a positive cash flow of $355, less expenses.

With these two properties in escrow, I felt like it was a good first trip and headed home. It took about two months for the loans to be processed and finally close escrow on both of the properties. These two properties were the first two I purchased and are classic 'no money down' deals. The theory is that you or the seller borrow the money that the seller needs to get from the sale and have him carry the balance on a trust deed, usually 20% or more. The ideal case would be in excess of 25%. This of course means that the first mortgage must be less than 50% if the seller expects to get anything after the Realtors commission and closing costs. On both of these deals I paid half of the closing costs.

To make deals like these work, your credit must be squeaky clean and lenders want to see some cash reserves someplace. My cash reserves were in a mutual fund and in my company's retirement account. My job was also very secure and all of my overtime was counted as income. (If you need to qualify for a home loan, whether it be for an investment or owner occupied, it always helps that when the loan company sends your employer the 'verification of employment' form, that you talk to the people who are going to fill it out just to make sure that all of your income is stated. This will keep it from having to be done over again. This is especially true when there's overtime or bonuses involved.)

In the event that you have no money, no job, no credit or any combination of the above, the same strategy for buying

George A. Cave

houses will work. The difference being, instead of <u>you</u> taking out the loan on the property, ask the <u>seller</u> to take out the loan and then you can assume it in escrow. This satisfies both parties, because you get the house and the seller gets the money he needs. The seller would also have to pay all of the closing cost, because you have no money.

In the case of FHA loans, there is no qualification to assume these loans. (Assumption meaning that you, the buyer, are assuming the responsibility of the loan, its payment, and all other provisions of the mortgage.) This is going to be a little bit more difficult but you will still be able to find plenty of sellers that will be willing to do it this way, especially in a slow moving market when the seller needs to liquidate quickly. This is especially true if the seller has bought another home or his job has been transferred elsewhere and he has to move quickly. You would be surprised what a motivated seller will do to move his property when he needs to.

(This type of 'no money down' deal even works well when working with Realtors. I've asked Realtors to merely print me out a list of all houses in the area that were in my price range with a mortgage of less than 50% and an owner willing to carry a second mortgage himself. It's amazing how many properties you could buy like this.)

Now that I bought my first two properties, I would like to go over several of the mistakes that I made in the hope that you won't make those same mistakes. Both properties sounded like the deals were fine, however, there was a major flaw in them both. That flaw being a balloon payment. A balloon payment is when, as in this case, no payments are made until a predetermined time in the future. Sometimes progress

An Intelligent Approach To Buying Real Estate

payments are made, sometimes interest and/or some principal is paid but it is not fully amortized and there's a balance due when the loan matures. In both of these cases, there were no progress payments made but interest was accumulating. The theory is that by the time the balloon payment is due the property will have appreciated, gone up in value. I would be then able to refinance the properties and pay off the loans.

Now, if you feel that time is going too slow in your life and it just seems to drag by, get a balloon payment and you will be amazed at how fast time fly's by. In the case of the duplex, the balloon was due in just three years and the properties in that area went down in value instead of up and I didn't have the money to pay off the note. This was not a big setback in that I had already made really good monthly income with no out of pocket expenses.

The duplex was new when I bought it so there was virtually no fix up and both units stayed rented for the entire time. When I couldn't come up with the money to pay off the owner carryback and the seller was not willing to re-negotiate the note, I gave him a 'Deed in Lieu of Foreclosure', giving him the property back. He paid off the first mortgage himself, so he once again owned it free and clear. This was the loan that I had taken out and since the owner paid it in full, my name was no longer on it and it appeared as if I had paid it off.

Luckily for me, this foreclosure, since it was to a private individual and not a mortgage company, did not appear on my credit report and therefore did me no harm at all. This is the case with most owner carrybacks, they don't report them to credit reporting agencies so there was no harm done to my credit and since the first mortgage was paid off there was no

George A. Cave

evidence that I ever owned the property. I would much rather have fully amortized the owner carryback and not have had this problem come up in the first place.

Another way to alleviate the problem of a balloon payment, yet still keep a good cash flow, (that's why the carryback was set up the way it was so that I could have a decent cash flow), is to graduate the payments. Remember that the terms of an owner carryback can be anything that you and the seller agree to. Graduated payments would step the payment up as the rents go up, (property values may fluctuate but rents have a tendency to only go up).

So instead of no payments for a certain amount of time, it might be just a year or two, (go as long as the seller will permit and you'll probably be surprised how long he will permit) and then give him a token amount, maybe $25 a month. Then each year raise it another $25 until it's paid off. So the first year that payments are due the monthly payment would be $25. The next year the monthly payment would be $50. The following year the monthly payment would be $75 and so on. This is merely one example of the graduated payment loan. Again, you can make up any terms that you and the seller agree to.

One problem with making payments that don't cover all of the interest is that the loan amount continues to increase. This is not good for you if you are the <u>buyer</u>. (It's good for the seller, so if <u>you are the seller</u> insist on getting paid interest for any note that you may be carrying.) If you are the buyer, ask that no interest accumulate over the monthly payment amount. So while no payments are being made, there would be no interest charged. As the payments are made, ask that the

An Intelligent Approach To Buying Real Estate

monthly payment fully satisfy any interest that may accumulate. This way the loan amount will never go up. (Don't feel that you have to remember all of these things right away. A good escrow officer will be able to work out the details. Just tell him what it is you are trying to accomplish, no negative amortization, and she should be able to take care of the rest.)

The first house that I bought had a balloon payment as well, but it wasn't due for five years. By the time it became due the loan amount had risen from the original amount of $15,000 to around $23,000, due to the interest that was accumulating and not being paid down monthly. This property decreased in value as well, and again I couldn't secure new financing to pay it off. (I had started investing in real estate at one of the worst possible times. Home values had peaked and over the next several years decreased in price.

At the time of this writing home prices are starting to increase again in many parts of the country, making it an excellent time to invest.) What I had hoped to do was to re-negotiate the terms to pay it off over a period of time, but again the seller felt he could do better to take it back. So once again I gave the seller a 'Deed in Lieu of Foreclosure'. This one worked out a little bit differently in that the second mortgage that I had taken out was unassumable, meaning that if I sold the property, or it changed ownership as it had in this case, it became fully due and payable. However, in the case of a foreclosure by the third mortgagee, it was assumable.

Several months after giving it back to the seller, I got a letter from the mortgage company of the second mortgage saying that they were going to foreclose because the property had been transferred to another name. I called them up and

George A. Cave

explained that they couldn't do that because the property had already been foreclosed on. They informed me that everything would be fine except that the new owner, the original seller, had not returned the necessary paperwork to transfer the loan into his name. At this point I felt that the seller had problems and may now be willing to talk about terms on the note.

I was correct. When I called him, I acted as if I didn't know anything was wrong except that Wells Fargo was going to foreclose. He asked me if I would be willing to repurchase the property. I told him that I still didn't have any money to put down. (I always tell people that and by this time I had quite a bit of cash reserves but still feel that each property has to stand on it's own and rather than spend thousands of dollars on a property that has decreased in value I would just as soon go buy something else. This is one reason that a positive cash flow is so desirable. Coupled with no out of pocket money to purchase the property makes it very easy to walk away from a deal that has gone bad. In both of these houses my credit was not damaged at all and I made good money off of the properties as long as I owned them.) He asked if I could put together a couple of thousand dollars and he'd carry a note for the rest.

Before we were done with the negotiations, instead of me paying him the $23,000 that the note was for, I gave him $3,000 now and agreed to pay him another $3,000 in three years with no interest and no payments being due. Since I had given him back the property, I looked upon this reaquisition as a new purchase and therefore got it back at an excellent price, approximately $9,000 less than I originally paid for it and $5,000 under its current value. If I had a choice I wouldn't

An Intelligent Approach To Buying Real Estate

have paid him any cash at all but I was concerned that Wells Fargo would indeed foreclose if I didn't get the property back, and they had every intention of doing so.

I had to call Wells Fargo back to let them know that I was once again the owner of the property and that there was no need for them to continue with the foreclosure. The woman that I spoke with at Wells Fargo said that the terms of the loan said that if the property changed names, they could foreclose, and now it had changed names again. I again explained that I was the one who took out the original loan and so now there was no reason to foreclose. She again said that the property had now changed hands twice and they were going to continue with the foreclosure. I suggested that they may feel a little foolish taking this before a judge when I was the one who took out the loan. At this she saw that it was ridiculous to continue and that in court I would probably win. She then said "Okay, we won't foreclose, but we're going to be keeping an eye on you". I had no idea what she meant by that but it appeared to make her feel better so I let it go.

The other problem with this house was that it was old and it had an addition put on it that had a flat roof. (Flat roofs are often difficult to maintain.)The age of the house meant that something was always going wrong with it and it would generally cost me about $750 a year to maintain it even with the excellent tenants that I had. They would do many of the repairs themselves.

Finally, after nine years, the tenants moved out and I decided that the maintenance was to high, so rather than rent it out again, I decided to sell it. The house sold in 30 days at a price of $20,000 more than I paid for it.

George A. Cave

So even though both properties were a learning experience they both made me money. Again, before buying any piece of property, know what it is that you are going to do with it. Make your money up front, that is, get a better than decent price and terms, and don't ever get yourself into a balloon payment of less than seven years and then always add a clause that if the value does not support a refinance of the property then the loan will convert to an amortized loan. It is best to stay away from balloon payments altogether until you become more experienced with them.

As these two stories unfolded I went and purchased dozens of other properties. Having learned from my mistakes, I was not about to make them again. In the next chapter we will talk about buying foreclosures.

Chapter Five

BUYING FORECLOSURES

VA Foreclosures:

As I was searching for houses to buy in Phoenix I noticed several ads in the newspaper about buying government properties. The books that I had been reading also said that government-owned homes were some of the best deals around. I called some of the agents and finally asked one of them to look at some of the properties that met with my criteria, let me know where they were and I'd go take a look at them the next time I was in town. The Veterans Administration was selling the properties that they had foreclosed on for nothing down

George A. Cave

with 100% financing, fixed rate for 30 years. This was the same loan that they gave to veterans but anyone could buy them. I put offers in on six properties and none of them were accepted by the government. After a while I asked to see the criteria for purchasing the properties and my agent was more than happy to send it to me.

After reviewing the material, I discovered that the agent had not been following the rules set down by the VA. It was to become my experience that no matter how stupid the requirement seemed, the government will not even look at your offer if any part of the paperwork was not in proper order. This was another perfect example of a so-called specialist in her field who was not very good.

The next month I went out to Phoenix and got a list of homes offered for sale by the Veterans Administration and selected the ones that met with my initial criteria. The cost had to be less than $50,000. They also had to be in a certain part of town. Once I had taken my first cut at the list I would plot them out on a map of Phoenix and go out and see them. The first list had about twenty homes to look at.

The next round of cuts dealt with what kind of condition was the house in. I was looking for virtually move-in condition, as well as a nice quiet neighborhood. I also didn't want anything on a busy street. If a house met all of my criteria, I would take a Polaroid picture of it and label the picture with the address. I would also take notes on all of the houses that I would visit whether I was interested or not. This turned out to be quite useful in that all of the houses on the availability list would not be sold and might still be on the next

An Intelligent Approach To Buying Real Estate

list that came out. I would always check my "no way" list of previously viewed homes before I made out the next map.

It took an entire day to see all of the houses on my list. Some houses I could just drive up to and tell right away that I didn't want to waste any time inside the house because the outside didn't meet my standards. This may have been something as simple as that it needed paint or the roof was in poor shape. If the outside was not in move-in condition there was no need to go any further.

Some of the houses told a sad story. You could see that there was a room being added on or a pool had just been put in and the people obviously got in over their head and couldn't make the payments. It was really quite sad in some cases. (This same sort of thing happened to my sister and her husband Shawn when he got out of the Air Force. They bought a brand new home with their GI Bill, then went out and bought all new furniture, a new car and did a lot of work in the yard. When the first mortgage payment came due, they didn't have the money. Shawn lost his job shortly after that, they had no money in the bank and never made a single payment on the house. It took the Veterans Administration over a year to foreclose.)

If the outside of the house met my standards, I would then proceed to the inside, often-times not going any further than looking in through the front window. I had no key to the houses and couldn't do a good inside check as I would have liked. But this was about to change.

I put in an offer on the house that I felt was the best I could find for my purposes. I followed the VA's instructions to the letter. I prepared the paperwork and handed it to the

George A. Cave

real estate agent, the one who was a professional in the field of government homes. All she had to do was walk it down to the Veterans building in downtown Phoenix and she evidently did this without any problems. My offer was accepted and I purchased the home. When it was all over and done with the property cost me about 2% of the purchase price to acquire after escrow fees (approximately 1%) and a 1 % loan point.

I also found out that the agent got a 5% commission. I decided to talk to a broker who had become a friend, who mostly dealt in vacant land, to see if he would be interested in working out an arrangement with me on the commission. I would do all of the leg work and paperwork and all he would have to do is take the completed paperwork package down to the VA building. In exchange we would split the commission 50/50. He agreed. He also loaned me his master key to the VA properties so that I could gain access to the properties without his being present.

By this time my mind was working overtime. I had already figured out how to get section 8 tenants (government subsidized leases) in less than a week and I also found that three bedroom homes would rent out the fastest, for about five-hundred dollars per month. I then targeted homes under $50,000, with many being bought at under $30,000. A $50,000 mortgage would have a maximum monthly payment of $430, including principle, interest, taxes and insurance (PITI). There didn't seem to be much rationale in how the Veterans Administration selected a purchase price because very often the less expensive homes were in better shape and were more marketable than other homes costing thousands more.

An Intelligent Approach To Buying Real Estate

When I would put in an offer to the VA on one of their homes I would always add one percent to the purchase price so that I would have a better chance of beating out anyone else whose offer was close to mine. The Veterans Administration had a priority system that they worked on where the purchaser that was going to purchase the home for cash had first priority. They also discounted the price for a cash sale. Their next priority would be a purchaser that was going to live in the house. The last priority was the investor that was going to finance the entire amount. In other words, I was last on their priority list.

I would try to find two houses out of any given list that met my criteria and put in offers on both of them. I would usually get one house or the other but never both of them- until the month that I purchased five.

The way my program would work is simply like this. I would find a home for say $50,000. My out of pocket expenses would be $1,000 to purchase the home. My half of the commission would be $1,250. The VA would notify me sometimes 60 days before the close of escrow that my offer had been accepted. Along with this notice came the closing date. If a property closed at the end of the month my out-of-pocket expenses were less due to the prorated interest. If the closing date was too soon or towards the first of the month I would have the broker reschedule the closing date in an attempt to keep my out-of-pocket expenses to a minimum and give me time to do what I needed to do.

As soon as I got the notification from the VA that my offer had been accepted and had a closing date, I went ahead and did whatever work needed to be done (and remember it had to be very minor) and moved a tenant into the house usually a month, or more, before the property closed. Remembering that rent is paid on the first of the month for the up-coming month and the mortgage payments are made on the first of the month for the previous month. (That is to say that the mortgage payments are made in arrears and rent is paid in advance.)

This would mean that in a best case scenario I would collect three months rent before the first mortgage payment was due. The final outcome in a purchase that went entirely by my plan would mean that I would get $1,250 from my half of the commission, and $1,000 from the rent before I had to start making mortgage payments for a total of $2,250. With costs at $1,000 for closing costs and loan origination fee and about $250 in repairs and miscellaneous expenses, leaving me with a net gain in my pocket of $1,000 to purchase a house. I would then have a positive cash flow, tax breaks and future appreciation.

The month that I purchased five houses in one month was when the VA decided that they were going to start charging investors a five percent down payment. They had given us plenty of warning of this change in policy giving me ample of time to put in as many offers as I could before the date of the policy change.

Several years later the Veterans Administration once again offered properties to investors with no money down and I once again started to buy properties using this method as did several of my friends. I always caution anyone contemplating the investment of real estate that it is not a static investment. It lives and breathes and will reward you over and over again if you are willing to put in the time and patience required to do the job right. The biggest problem with real estate is tenants and if you're not prepared to deal with them hire someone to do it or invest in something else.

At the time of this writing the VA requires a down payment of five percent for anyone who is going to occupy the home. Again, these are VA foreclosures and you don't have to be a veteran to buy one. Using a little ingenuity one could see right away that a person could purchase a home from the VA as an owner-occupant, live in it for a little while and then go buy another home from the VA, live in it for awhile, etc. Get the picture? This sort of strategy would work very well for someone who is looking to purchase a home every six months to a year.

For investors, you would be required to put down five percent as well, (this may vary on what part of the country that you live in). Still, under my plan it makes real estate investing quite simple even with the five percent down. Several people that I know are still very happy with the simplicity of this plan even with having to put down the five percent. Using the previous scenario it would cost an investor about $2,750 to purchase a $50,000 house. The VA changes the rules from time to time and you never know when they may once again sell to investors for 'no money down'.

FHA Foreclosures:

FHA foreclosures are very similar to VA foreclosures. The FHA has a minimum bid that is probably very close to the value of the property. The FHA also finances the properties themselves on many of the properties but also have an equal number of properties that the FHA will not finance themselves or through a FHA lender. In these cases the buyer must secure conventional financing or pay cash. These houses are usually in need of major repair but for the seasoned investor they can be very lucrative.

The qualifications for purchasing a foreclosed home through the FHA are the same as qualifying for an FHA loan from an authorized lender, that being: two years in the same line of work, two years since the filing of a bankruptcy. Three years for any foreclosures of property that you own, reasonably good credit with no bills currently at collections, and an income to mortgage ratio that shows that you could afford the monthly payment.

As you start to amass more and more properties you'll see that financing them may become increasingly difficult. It seems that the more properties you have the more nervous it makes lenders. Some lenders won't lend money even on a personal residence if the borrower has more than five homes. We will see in the next chapter how your real estate empire can be kept somewhat secret.

Conventional Foreclosures:

Entire books are written about buying foreclosures from conventional lending institutions. I don't intend to go into every detail of buying foreclosures, but instead I want give you my experiences with buying foreclosures from REO's, (Real Estate Owned) that is conventional lenders.

An Intelligent Approach To Buying Real Estate

Foreclosures are some of the best deals that can be found. Tens of thousands of dollars can be made if you can acquire the property before the lender forecloses. This type of buying usually involves a significant amount of cash on hand. But if you have access to the money it can be quite lucrative.

Many distressed owners advertise to sell their homes themselves and will place ads in the newspaper stating that they are a motivated seller. Dealing with them is the same as with any other distressed seller. But in the case of people who are behind in their payments, they have to get money now or lose everything. If you have the cash that they need and enough money to make up the back payments, very often the seller will walk away from his equity. Again, this is the best time to get a foreclosure, <u>before</u> it actually happens, and from the owner, not the bank.

Many people who buy properties that are going to foreclosure will run ads in the newspaper themselves to find a seller. These ads would read something like this; "I buy houses for cash, within 24 hours", or "Behind in payments, in foreclosure, I buy houses for cash", "In foreclosure, get cash today". (Don't forget to place your phone number in the ad.)

Buying foreclosures from lending institutions can be very advantageous also. Every lender is different and what I have done is simply call lenders over the phone and ask to speak with their REO. If I don't have the right phone number they usually can give it to me. Very often they will have a real estate broker handling this for them. I have bought several foreclosures from institutional lenders and have never paid more than a 5% down payment. I've also gotten some very good deals from them. I bought two three bedroom condominiums from a bank that was asking $35,000 a piece for them. I felt that this was already a good price, but I asked for a sale price of $25,000 and they accepted it without an argument. Makes me wish I had offered them less. Both of these places rent out for $550 a month and the payment is less than $230 a month (P&I).

I've also seen lenders advertise in the local newspaper. They almost always finance the properties themselves and at a very reasonable rate with a low down payment. In the foreclosures that I have done, the lender has been very agreeable to whatever I have asked for. They have even done repairs on the units for me before I took possession of the units and sometimes they will reduce the amount of the down payment required if you agree to do the necessary repairs.

When buying foreclosures from institutional lenders, keep in mind that they are not in the real estate business. They are in the lending money business and really don't want to be bothered with the sale or management of real estate, so they would like to get rid of it as quickly as possible. They also need to keep the number of units that they have foreclosed on to a minimum. Every lender is different but if you have the time to call around and check on the motivation of the lenders, it could be worth your while.

Chapter Six

CREATIVE BUYING

I found out early in my real estate investing that buying houses was like dating, that's right - dating. You're not going to get anywhere if you don't ask. In real estate, the worst that can happen is you'll be told no. Sounds like dating to me!

"He Who Cares Least Wins."

Once you get into the realm of investing you will be shocked at what people will be willing to do. I purchased several homes with no money, no financing, no qualifying, no escrow fees, no out of pocket expenses at all. These were properties that the owner just wanted to get rid of and they were prepared to merely sign them over to me. Again, don't accept a house even in this manner without taking the necessary amount of safe guards. The least that you would want to do is to go through escrow so you could get a preliminary title report and title insurance.

It would do you no good to have someone give you their home just to find out when you go to sell it that there's a tax lien or a judgment against the previous owner and all of a sudden those debts get paid off before you do. (Title insurance insures that there are no claims to the title other than what is recorded. They issue a report, a preliminary title report, of the status of the title and if there are any problems, they will not insure it. This type of title insurance is necessary, remembering that a deed does not have to be filed to be valid. I say again - a deed does not have to be filed to be valid. So if a dubious seller gave someone else a title as well it could cause problems later on. With title insurance, the problem won't be yours.)

Let me explain further. If a person gets sued or has a judgment against them from court, whether it be for child support, nonpayment of a contractual agreement, or any type of tax lien (IRS, state, property, etc.) they would undoubtedly put a lien on any property that person might own. Then, that person gives you the property and you are now placed on the title _after_ the lien. The lien gets paid before you do if you decide to sell the property.

This is not to discourage anyone from taking one of these types of deals, just have it checked out first through a title company. In all the houses that have been given to me, not a single title has had problems. So the chances may be slim but it is worth the time and expense to be safe. Don't take on any properties that are going to cause you problems later, they are just not worth it. There are too many good deals out there to get involved in one that will cause you headaches later.

An Intelligent Approach To Buying Real Estate

Remember that in order for a deal to go down the buyer's needs must be met. In a lot of instances it's nothing more than paying his share of the escrow costs. Other times they would feel a lot better if they got some kind of down payment. This is in the case where you don't want to secure financing and want to take full advantage of what is already in place. (This is called a "cash to mortgage", CTM. There are always plenty of these advertised in the newspaper and the cash part is negotiable. They may be asking for "$5,000 and take over loan", but they might settle for $2,000.) This has worked for me in Phoenix and California and therefore will work anywhere in the country.

Next, I started buying condominiums in Phoenix and several owners wanted to sell at any cost. Condos don't do very well in Phoenix and the prices were falling fast. The first condo I purchased in this particular complex cost me $45,000 and I felt it was a great buy. The rooms were all nice-sized, the complex was really nice and the rent paid the mortgage. (This was one of those 0% downs from the VA.)

Eight years later I'm buying units in that same complex for $20,000. Sound depressing? No. Why? Simple, my rent still pays for that one that I paid at the height of the market and the rents have done nothing but go up.

Some owners in this complex have moved into houses or out of the area and can't sell their unit. One owner owned his unit free and clear, no mortgage. He sent me a letter asking if I would be interested in purchasing his unit for $15,000, with terms. (This happens quite often, once you get involved with real estate investing. People will tell others and they will call

George A. Cave

you.) I telephoned and offered him 10% down, ($1,500) and he'd carry the balance at eight percent for 15 years.

He called me back and asked if I could give him $2,000 down and have the loan amortized over 7 years. A little quick math showed that my monthly payment would be only $202 a month for 7 years and then the property would be completely paid for. The rent would be in excess of $450 a month and the homeowners fees were $100 a month leaving me with a positive cash flow of over $100 dollars a month after figuring in maintenance and vacancy. (Maintenance on condominiums is less than houses because the homeowners association is responsible for the exterior maintenance of the building.) That gives me a net return on my investment of 60% annually and in seven years the mortgage will be paid off and I'll get a $202 a month increase giving me a 185% annual return on my original $2,000 investment, even if the rent doesn't go up and it will. SOLD. (The mortgage that we created was between the seller and me and not a lending institution. Therefore it was not put on my credit report.)

Others are willing to sell their property very similarly, but maybe they have more equity and are not willing to just let it go. I then offer them a very small down payment, only two or three thousand dollars, and have the owner carry a note for the difference of the balance of the purchase price and the amount of the mortgage. For instance, a house is being sold for $55,000. I offer the seller $50,000 (I generally ask for 10% less than what they are asking, sometimes more.), the seller owes $40,000 and needs $2,000 down. I give him the $2,000, assume the payments on the loan, (this keeps the loan in his name and not in mine), and we create a second trust deed for

An Intelligent Approach To Buying Real Estate

the balance of $8,000. This is where the negotiating starts because I want to pay as little on that second mortgage as possible. The first mortgage is fixed and there's nothing I can do about that. So I ask the owner to carry the second for some length of time without interest or payments and then amortize it over a long period of time. I generally start by asking for ten years with no payment or interest. (There's nothing more frustrating than asking for a period of time without payments or interest and the seller accept it without an argument. At that I always wonder how much longer he would have gone.) Again, it's like dating, if you don't ask!

I like to start by explaining that my motivation is to collect the rent and I will have to have a positive cash flow and with the current market it may difficult to make ends meet or for me to make any return on my investment. (Remember, you must satisfy the seller's needs and that $2,000 down payment is supposed to do that. This carryback is something that he is probably not counting on right away and his desire to sell the house is more important than his desire to make $80 a month on the note, for now anyway.) Very often the seller will agree immediately and I will have wished I asked for a longer time without payments and interest. Sometimes that seller will say something like, "I can't go that long without payments and interest". My response would then be, "Well, how long can you go"? You might then suggest eight years or maybe seven. With this type of strategy it doesn't matter. I'm ready to pay him for his note starting right now but then I would ask for the amortization to be longer and the interest rate will be less trying to negotiate a lower payment.

George A. Cave

If you have a lot of cash to put down you might make the seller a ridiculously low offer to cash him out. This works well if you are planning to turn the property around for a quick sale and pocket the profit. This has worked out fine for me in the past and will always continue to do so. The more money that you have, the better prices you can get real estate.

A lot of the properties I've purchased, owners will go five years without payments or interest before I have to start making payments on the loan. It is important that if you're not going to make payments on the loan, don't let the interest accrue. This just increases your indebtedness so you may want to rethink it. Every deal is different so it's important to think the entire transaction through. Any decent sized book store will sell amortization books with nothing but loan schedules to help you figure out what a loan payment is going to be at a specific interest rate over a set number a years. There are several computer programs that will calculate payments as well. I use Quicken. There is also a table in the back of this book that will be helpful.

I always indicate on the purchase contract that I will assume the <u>payments</u>. I don't specifically state that I am not assuming the loan, the loan will stay in the name of the seller. This will make some sellers nervous, me, for instance. I sell properties completely different from the way I purchase them. When I sell a property and my name is on the loan, I insist that the buyer assume the loan and the guarantee, if it has one, or secure new financing. In the case where I assume the payments and my name isn't on the loan, I will allow the new buyer to do the same thing.

An Intelligent Approach To Buying Real Estate

In the case of the house described above, I may want to turn around and resell that house. So now I have a house with a $40,000 first, lets say at 8% and a second for $8,000 at 7% (always ask the seller for a lower interest rate than what is currently available because whatever the current rate is, it's always too high) leaving a balance owed of $48,000. The payment on the first is $415 (PITI) with 15 years left to pay and there is no payment on the second for five years. Then the payment on the second is $92 a month, fully amortized over the next ten years, for a total of $507 a month. (In this case, the entire house would be paid off in 15 years.)

I might decide to sell that house for $60,000, with $5,000 down and I will 'wrap' the mortgage, now at $55,000. The new buyer and I decided upon an interest rate of 8 1/2 % for 15 years making the payment $591 a month. The new seller sends one monthly payment in the amount of $591 to the title company each month. The title company then sends out two payments for the first five years. One in the amount of $415 to the first mortgage holder and the balance of $176 a month to me. After five years, my portion will reduce by $92 a month because the payment on the second trust deed is now due every month. The entire loan is fully amortized over the length of the existing loans. I get $2,000 in my pocket and an income of $176 a month for five years and then $84 a month for the next ten years and I don't have to worry about tenants, or maintenance. If the buyer defaults I can foreclose on him and do the whole thing all over again from the beginning.

I will however put a 'due on sale clause' into the purchase contract so if the buyer wishes to sell the property, I will be paid off entirely. The second trust deed that the original seller

George A. Cave

is carrying is still open for negotiation. If you have some cash to invest before the note becomes due for payments, you might want to ask the holder of that $8,000 note if he would be willing to sell it at a discount, in this case maybe $3,000. He may not go for it but chances are he still needs money and $3,000 in hand may be more appealing to him than $92 a month. For you, it is very appealing in that you just acquired an $8,000 note and deed of trust for $3,000 and you will continue to receive the $92 a month for a net return of 37% annually. Not too bad.

Buying a discounted note has also worked for me when I knew that a house I owned was going to sell. The original owner, who carried back the second, doesn't know that I'm selling the house and I offer to buy the note from him. It costs me no money out of my pocket because he'll be paid off from the funding of a new loan through escrow. So instead of a monthly payment, I pick up an additional $5,000 in cash, right now.

This very thing happened on a very nice home I purchased and kept for only a few months. The new buyer secured a new loan to pay off the first mortgage, the note and deed of trust that the previous owner was carrying for me when I bought it, and the equity that I had in the house. (I bought the house for about $15,000 under market and was still selling it for $5,000 under market, making a profit of $10,000 for myself.) The previous owner was carrying a note for $12,000 with no payments or interest for 7 years, and I asked him if he would be willing to sell it at a discount. Without me so much as making him an offer he discounted the note 40%, ($4,800). So instead of just the $10,000 I was going to make, I got an

An Intelligent Approach To Buying Real Estate

additional $4,800 from the discounting of the second and the original owner knew nothing about it and even if he did he probably wouldn't care because he was going to get $7,200 right now instead of having to wait seven years to start getting a small monthly check. (In this case the "first right of refusal clause", that I always insert in an owner carryback, would guarantee that you are the one who is going to reap the discount, in this case $4,800.)

This type of transaction is for the experienced investor and if you're not sure about how to do it or whether it is right for you, simply ask your escrow officer. A good escrow officer can help you purchase a great deal of real estate and make you lots of money. They will do everything from writing up the purchase contract to servicing the owner financing. You will definitely want to make the payments on an owner carryback through a title or escrow company. (It will usually have to be the title/escrow company that you used to close the deal. They are not in the business to service loans so they will only provide this service to their customers.) You would send the monthly payment to them and they would in turn send out a separate check to each of the lien holders. They act as a distributor of the money and they keep very close track of the interest and principal of the loan and send out the tax information to both parties. They charge about $7 a month for this service, usually split between the buyer and the seller, and it is well worth the money. The title/escrow company also retains the reconveyance for the note when it's paid off or in the event, for some reason, the holder of the note can't be found or wishes to be unreasonable.

George A. Cave

This next one is a classic 'no money down' deal that I did in California on a house that appraised at $225,000. These strategies work in all price ranges and all areas of the country. This story is from my first book, "The Beast Next Door". The book is about how I bought the house from my former neighbors Andy and Pam, which happened to be next door to my ex-wife and her new husband. I had been living in an apartment and was looking around for something to buy close to our children.

Andy and Pam had become very good friends and they were attempting to sell their house. The thought of me purchasing it had never really occurred to me. Andy had accepted a new job in Oregon and was anxious to sell his place. He was attempting to sell it "by owner" and was not having much success. I wasn't in any hurry to buy anything and was waiting for what I thought was the perfect deal.

One weekend while having a barbecue with the neighbors across the street, the topic of selling his house came up and Andy suggested that I buy it. I told him that he wouldn't like the way I buy houses and left it at that.

A few days later while I was at my old house (the one where my ex-wife and her new husband where living) tending to my birds. (I raise exotic birds, again that is better explained in "The Beast Next Door"). Andy came over and again asked me if I would buy his house. This time I took him seriously and started to think about it. I had been in his house and knew that it was in need of complete remodeling. I asked what kind of price he was looking for and he said he just wanted to get back what he had paid for it. Now, this was the kind of talk that I liked to hear.

An Intelligent Approach To Buying Real Estate

"OK Andy, how much did you pay for it"? This was the start of real negotiations. I don't think Andy really knew what was about to hit him but he answered the question. "$193,000". That wasn't too bad a price since they were selling for over $225,000. Even with all the work that I was going to have to do which I felt would cost about $10,000, I felt that this was a good price. I told Andy that I would 'attempt' to purchase the house; however I would be putting "no money down".

Andy had a first mortgage of $145,000 and he needed some cash out of it to pay back his Uncle Pat for lending him part of the down payment. I told him that we would establish a selling price of $193,000, and I would apply for a loan for 75-80% of the appraised value of $225,000. He would have to be happy with whatever cash came out of that loan after the mortgage was paid off. The difference between the new loan amount and the actual selling price of $193,000 would be carried in a second trust deed by him for five years with graduated payments. The first year there would be no payments. The second year there would be a payment of $100 per month, the next year the payment would go to $200 per month and increase by $100 every year until the balance was due in five years. Andy would also be paying all of the closing costs and any loan fees.

Andy agreed to this deal. It was about as fair as I could come up with but Andy had to run everything by his Uncle Pat. Uncle Pat is a dentist who, Andy says, is a real estate buff. Uncle Pat is why Andy felt that he could sell the house without the use and expense of a real estate broker. I hoped that Uncle Pat was a better dentist than he was a Realtor.

George A. Cave

I felt that I didn't have anything to lose. If I got the house, that was fine and if I didn't I would go find something else. The more I thought about it the more I liked the idea of living next door to my children. I felt that this would be the perfect set up for me to see them whenever I wanted to. This would actually help out their mother, too in that I would be available for baby-sitting if she wanted to go out. I would also be right next door to my bird collection and could expand the collection into my new backyard giving me twice the room and twice the number of birds. The only drawback was that I hadn't talked it over with my ex-wife yet.

There had been no reason to say anything to her up until now, but when we started escrow I felt it was time to run it past her. At first she didn't see anything wrong with the idea at all, but after she had some time to think it over she started back-pedalling.

"Never Spend Your Money Before You Get It"

She suggested that I purchase a home a few blocks away. She felt that would be close enough to see the boys regularly but she wouldn't have to see my fiancee every day. I explained that we were not going to be coming over for dinner every night and that I do have a constitutional right to live where ever I please so - "Get used to it."

Andy and Pam moved out of the house and up to Oregon to start their new jobs. They were anxious to close escrow on this house because they were now making two house payments, the one in Oregon where they were now living, and on the one that I was going to buy. The escrow on the house

An Intelligent Approach To Buying Real Estate

was progressing as planned. The appraisal on the house came in exactly as I had hoped at $225,000. I got loan approval at 75% of the appraisal which came to $168,000. There had been some talk that I may have been able to get approved for an 80% loan which would have given Andy another $10,000 but this was the best I could get.

It turns out that Andy had already been counting on the extra ten grand and so was his Uncle Pat. When the loan came in approved at $168,000 he was disappointed. Here's another important business tip, "Never spend your money before you get it."

The evening before we were supposed to close escrow, I was just getting ready to go to bed when the phone rang. It was Andy. He had been talking with Uncle Pat and they decided that they weren't going to sign the final escrow papers unless I gave them the difference of the $10,000 in cash. I told Andy that we had agreed on the terms, that I tried to get the 80% loan value but was not able to, and that he had already agreed to the lower amount in the event that was all I could get.

"Well Uncle Pat doesn't feel that I'm getting out of the house what it's worth."

"You're going to get the same amount of money, you're just going to have to wait for the extra $10,000. So, call Uncle Pat and tell him that I am not going to put in $10,000 in cash."

Andy called me back a little while later and said the Uncle Pat suggested that we make a separate note for the $10,000, instead of adding it to the second that Andy was going to carry anyway, and have it due in one year.

George A. Cave

I told Andy that I was not going to spend $10,000 to fix the house up just so I could give him another $10,000 in a year. Also what would happen if I didn't have the $10,000 next year? I would end up spending $10,000 to fix up the house just so he could foreclose on me. Not a very bright thing to do. Andy decided to call Uncle Pat again.

A few minutes later, Andy called back to tell me that Uncle Pat said that if I didn't agree to the terms then we didn't have a deal. I told Andy that I was approved for a loan in the amount of $168,000. The house didn't matter. I would merely go out and find a different house to buy. I further explained that his uncle was not the one making two house payments and if I didn't buy this house, who was going to? There wasn't exactly a line forming to get it. Andy stood fast.

I told Andy that the loan company was waiting and they expedited this loan because he was in a hurry. I was not going to stall the escrow now. If Andy did not sign the final paperwork, and have it faxed to the escrow company by noon tomorrow, I would cancel the escrow and find another house to buy. Then I went to bed.

I normally get up about 7:00 AM to get to work by 8:00 but the next morning I was awakened by the phone at six o'clock. It was Andy. All he said was "I couldn't sleep at all last night. I've signed the paperwork and faxed it back to the escrow company. F_ _ _ Uncle Pat."

Here's another tip when investing in anything. "He who cares least, wins". This is also why I would not move into the house before I owned it. If I had moved into the house I might have made an emotional commitment that would have clouded my judgment. We closed escrow that day. I ended up

An Intelligent Approach To Buying Real Estate

purchasing a $225,000 house for $193,000, with no money out of my pocket. How it was done was a standard 25 percent down purchase with a new conventional loan. The trick was to get my down payment back. That was accomplished by the seller giving me a loan immediately after escrow closed. All the paperwork was signed prior to the close of escrow, so my money never left the escrow company. There is no provision in my mortgage that says I can't immediately go out and take out a loan against my home. In this case it was done ten minutes after the new loan funded.

The biggest problem with buying a house in this manner is that I had to come up with the down payment to run through escrow. Even though I was going to get it back in a few days it had to appear as if I was putting that money down. The loan company will insist that they see where the money is coming from and that it is in escrow. Luckily for me I was able to have that much money available for the few days it took to close the deal. This type of purchase is not for the squeamish or soft hearted and is not recommended until you have a thorough knowledge of real estate and even then it was still the escrow officer who masterminded the entire transaction. I told him what I wanted to do and he came up with an even better plan.

In a deal like this it isn't uncommon to get cash back at the close of escrow in the form of an allowance. In this case I needed to get Andy as much cash as possible but you could stipulate in the purchase contract that the owner gets back a 'decorating allowance of $3,000", or a landscaping allowance of $2,500. You decide on the allowance and on the amount. The loan company looks at this as a way for the buyer to come up with less of a down payment so they won't let you take a

George A. Cave

very large percentage of the down payment as an allowance, if they know about it. In this case it would have worked out beautifully. You might buy a house that's in need of a roof and you get an allowance for $3,500 and you put the roof on yourself for $1,500. Guess who gets to keep the rest?

There's a similar version to this type of purchase which has been dubbed the "double close". Where, instead of doing it all at once, the seller would actually deed his house over to the buyer, he would carry a second for his equity, in this case $45,000, but the note would not be filed at the county recorder, (a note does not have to be recorded to be valid). The escrow would close and I would take ownership of the house before applying for a loan. I would <u>then</u> refinance the house with the original seller, in this case Andy, being paid his $25,000 and the rest being held as a second just as was done. I have never done it this way, but it was what I had intended to do before the escrow officer suggested his way which worked out fine but I did have to show nearly $70,000 in escrow, the intended down payment and escrow fees, all of which I got back.

The double close method assumes that it's easier to qualify and fund a loan on a house that you already own. The drawback is that the owner has to deed the title of his house over to you and wait for his money. If you don't qualify for the refinancing it becomes very messy. This type of deal works better for multi-unit buildings, where the property's ability to repay the loan is more important than the owner's financial condition.

Then again if there's enough equity in a property, some lenders will lend money to anyone on the equity of that

An Intelligent Approach To Buying Real Estate

property. The seller may not know this making it easy for you to negotiate the deal.

Chapter Seven

TENANTS

The worst part of owning real estate is having to deal with tenants. A good tenant is worth his or her weight in gold. Too many landlords don't realize this until it's too late. When your tenant calls you with a problem, be prompt. If you were having the problem would you expect to wait for it to be resolved? I have a friend who was renting a house that, when it rained, the roof leaked so bad that one of the bedrooms was saturated with water, making it completely unusable. It wasn't long before he moved to a different house. This was the perfect example of an idiot landlord. He just lost a very good tenant for something that he's going to have to fix anyway. Treat your tenants as you would like to be treated but make sure that they perform as well.

I know several people that I got interested in buying real estate and they also bought some houses in Phoenix on the VA foreclosure plan I was currently working. (I like to find a method that works for me and stay with it as long as it keeps working.) I explain to everyone I talk to about real estate all of the things that you are reading about here but they don't listen. People are lured by the income potential, tax advantages and the prestige of being able to tell people that they own three or four houses. In some cases twenty five or even one hundred houses. Do you think that would impress that pain-in-the neck-boss that keeps giving you a hard time? It did mine, when one day he timidly asked me how many houses I owned and my response was, "seventeen". I purchased all seventeen of them in my first year of investing and from outside the state. Some of them I purchased, had them fixed up and sold them without ever laying my eyes on them. He later asked me if I would show him how to invest in real estate also. I was only to happy to help. This has been my philosophy from the beginning. I would help anyone who wanted to learn how to buy property, everything I know.

"Good Tenants Are Worth Their Weight In Gold"

Another thing I found out fairly early in my investing was that one of the reasons some people sell their income property is because of their tenants, which by the way, I inherited when I bought their property. I didn't know it at the time but the tenants were a real nightmare. If you buy a house with a lease in existence, you will inherit the lease as well. Be very careful to check all leases. However, in the case of a bad or late to pay tenant, it usually isn't very hard to throw them out. Here's another rule. If you don't have the temperament to evict someone, don't buy real estate with the intention of renting it out.

I recommend that if you get the slightest feeling that the current tenant living in a property that you are buying is going to cause you problems, have them removed prior to your closing escrow. With all the problems I've had with inherited tenants, I have all of them removed before I'll buy a house. I will then make sure that the house is in the condition that it appeared to be in and put my own tenant in, all before I own it.

"Keep Cash Reserves In The Amount Of Two Months Rent On Hand For Each House That You Own."

One of the things that you must remember about tenants is that you are not their parents. Don't let them treat you as such. I like to rent to people on a government subsidized lease program called "Section 8". It's a program where the government pays a portion of the rent for a family, sometimes all of it. These are usually single mothers, with a large majority of them on welfare. If they have a job, then the government decides how much they can afford to pay and the tenant sends that amount directly to me. I prefer for the government to pay the entire rent. That way I spend much less time trying collecting the share of the rent that the tenant is supposed to pay. But then any time is too much. The good thing about this program is that the government pays the rent on time and being from out of state it made the first of the month a whole lot less frustrating.

An Intelligent Approach To Buying Real Estate

Chasing the tenant around for the rent is not only common to the low income households. Some of my biggest problems were middle class income tenants. You want to establish the rules immediately and don't let them slide. Establish due dates and if the rent is not paid by then impose a late fee and collect it. As soon as an irresponsible tenant realizes that you are not serious about the rules he will walk all over you. So you've got to do what you say. It's kind of like raising children, it's sad to say it but it's true.

I believe that I've heard just about every excuse there is about why the rent is not paid or why it's going to be late. The problem is, the mortgage company doesn't care about the excuses or why I haven't collected the rent yet, they want their money, on time. I explain this to all new tenants right off so there's no mistake, the rent is due on the first of each month.

Some of these friends of mine that got involved in investing as I did just couldn't get it through their heads that some tenants don't always tell the truth and they would get so frustrated when they would catch them in a lie and they wouldn't admit it. I explained that you are not their parents and as long as you act like their parents they will treat you like this. It doesn't matter if they are telling you the truth or not, it doesn't matter. If they don't do as they as supposed to, when they are supposed to, they are gone. I don't care if they told you that a burglar kicked in the front door. I guarantee it was their irate boyfriend. The tenant gets to pay for the door.

In one case, the people who owned the property were really nice and they wanted to give the tenant all the chances in the world. Unfortunately it cost them almost ten thousand dollars to fix the house up after they finally got tired of hearing

George A. Cave

the excuses. This is not my idea of success in real estate investing and it could have been avoided. A couple of weeks lost rent is worth the time and trouble of finding a good tenant.

It's also a good idea to check up on your properties every so often. Not so much that you become a pest to the tenant but enough to know if something's going wrong. For instance, say you are renting to a family that keeps the yard clean and neat and then suddenly for some reason you find that it's not. Or a tenant that always pays their rent on time, and then they start to pay it a little bit later each month. This is a wake up call that something may be going wrong. It may simply be that the lawn mower broke. It might also be a lost job or an impending divorce. You need to know these things as soon as possible so you can take whatever action you need to. Most of the time a lost job or a divorce is not that big of a problem to the landlord because most good tenants realize that no matter where they live they will have to pay their rent.

Sometimes however, you find that when these types of things happen a vacancy is imminent. Again you want to know as soon as possible. Vacancies should be calculated into the "net operating income", that's what it's going to cost to run the property, excluding the mortgage. Vacancy should be calculated at about 5 percent of the monthly rent. I find that in three bedroom houses the rate is much, much lower but 5 percent is still the figure I use when calculating the net operating income. I've had houses rented to the same people for nine years, and they're still renting them. But it's better to be prepared for vacancies and not have them than to not be prepared and have them.

An Intelligent Approach To Buying Real Estate

For my out of state tenants I provide them with self addressed stamped envelopes to send me their portion of the rent. It may sound silly but I can't remember how many times I've been told that the rent was late because the tenant lost my address or didn't have any stamps. Sometimes it doesn't take much of an excuse for a tenant to be late on the rent. This is a really easy problem to remedy, and it works.

One of my worst experiences in real estate was when I had just started purchasing houses and had acquired seven of them. I would lay awake at night wondering if the tenants were going to pay their rent on time. I was buying on a shoestring budget and could not afford to have more than one or two vacant units a month. There was no reason for my anxiety and I would rationalize it away by saying to myself, "What's the chances of all those houses going vacant in one month?"

Then of course, one month it happened. Five out of the seven went vacant without a single notice. They just didn't pay the rent and were gone. I tell you these stories not to dissuade you from buying real estate but to be aware of the dangers and pitfalls. I recommend that you buy one house at a time, make sure the tenant is reliable and everything is going the way you expected before you venture out further. This of course depends on your financial status. Some people have the money to cover the loss of rent in this type of instance. I, on the other hand, did not. Most of my properties at the time had a positive cash flow and I knew that it was only a question of time before the cash reserves would be available for this type of event. (That's provided of course that I didn't spend the cash reserves on something else. A good rule is to keep cash reserves in the amount of two months rent on hand for each house that you own.) All of the properties that went vacant that month were once again rented out before the end of the month with reliable tenants that remained with me for years. The tenants that had moved were those inherited ones that I spoke of earlier.

This was almost twelve years ago and I haven't had more than two properties vacant at the same time since.

Finding Good Tenants:

To find good tenants I first ask my existing good tenants if they know someone who might be looking for a place to rent. If you are a good landlord, your tenants will be only to happy to help you out. The next thing I do is place an ad in the newspaper. If you do this it is important that you answer the phone when it rings. Perspective tenants generally won't leave a message and even if they do, while they are waiting for you to return their call, they are out looking at other units to rent.

"Tenants Are Not Family"

Be prompt in your meetings with tenants. I almost always put the address in the ad so that the tenant will know where the property is and can drive by and take a look at it before calling me. Insist on a significant security deposit but not so much that no one will be able to rent it. Check what the going rate is in your area for security deposits, and when the tenant moves out give it back to him. There's nothing that gives landlords a worse reputation than those scumbags that don't return security deposits by making up every excuse imaginable. My

An Intelligent Approach To Buying Real Estate

policy is that if a tenant stays with me for over three years, and the house is in decent shape, they get back all of their deposit.

After three years you are going to have to repaint the house, clean the carpet, exterminate and do a host of other maintenance items that are not the fault of the tenant. I know of landlords that charge a tenant $5 to tighten a loose door handle. This is criminal, don't be like that.

Another method to attract tenants is to place a sign on the front lawn or in the front window. It depends on the area of town that you live in whether or not this is a good idea. In a good area, this is the first thing I do after getting off the phone with my tenants asking for referrals. In an area that's not so good, I don't put up a sign because the chances are the people who will be passing by and reading it are not anyone that I would care to rent to. Signs attract the same type of people who are currently renting in the area around the unit. If you are happy with the neighborhood, put up a sign. If you're not happy with the area, don't put up a sign.

Remember, tenants are not family, don't treat them as such and they won't treat you like family either. I have many relatives that I love dearly but I would not rent to them. I also don't get too chummy with my tenants, it becomes extremely difficult to evict friends and family. Even if it doesn't get to that point, some people seem to think that the landlord, for no other reason than being the landlord, is loaded with money and what does it hurt if I'm late with the rent or I don't pay it every now and then.

One time I was going to a property I owned to collect the rent that was late, and as I walked up to the front door I overheard the husband telling his wife that I was making a fortune off of them. The truth was, I was making about $200 a month on that property, hardly a fortune. But then I was the one who took all the risk, I was the one who assumed the responsibility to provide decent, affordable housing to those who either didn't want to buy a home or couldn't afford to buy one. In reality, landlords do the tenant quite a service, <u>if they do it right</u>.

Respect your tenants and they will respect you. Most states have laws that protect tenants and landlords. It's best to get a copy of these laws before you start to buy rental properties. They vary greatly from state to state. Most Realtors will have copies of them or you can get them from your local bookstore. The short of it is, treat your tenants as you would wish to be treated, and expect them to treat you as you would treat your landlord.

Chapter Eight

REAL ESTATE AND THE IRS

One of the advantages of real estate investing is taxes. If you purchase a home as a personal residence the interest and property taxes are deductible. If you are an investor, then the interest, property taxes, insurance, homeowners fees, repairs, and depreciation are all deductible. There's a host of other deductions that can be taken as well. That would include <u>any</u> expenses related to the investment property, including but not limited to: travel expenses, meals, hotels, tools, education (in some instances, pertaining to the investment, maintenance and management of your property), books, magazines, newspapers and the list goes on and on.

George A. Cave

This is very helpful especially if you were going to buy these things anyway. I have many properties hundreds of miles away from my home and I write off every expense in the travel and upkeep of those properties. Before you start to get nervous about whether or not that's okay with the IRS, I've been audited four times and the IRS has not once denied a single expense declared on my real estate. My deductions are legitimate and documented and I take every single one of them.

When I first started investing I was apprehensive about taking too many deductions because I was afraid of being audited. I was making over $50,000 a year at my full time job, owned my own home and took the interest deduction on that. Even though I was making money each month from my rentals, I was taking enough deductions, mostly due to depreciation, to pay no income taxes at all. After my first audit I realized that there was nothing to be afraid of, as long as you can substantiate your expenses.

One of the greatest benefits of real estate investing is depreciation. Depreciation is a deduction for the gradual deterioration of the structure but not the land upon which it sits. The theory is that over a period of time the structure will become worthless. In some instances this may be true but none of the properties I have will have to be rebuilt in the next 50 years. This is provided that the necessary repairs and upkeep are maintained, which also are tax deductible. The beautiful thing about depreciation is that you don't have to spend money to get it, like you must do for all other deductions. The interest, taxes, repairs, etc. are all deductions <u>after</u> you spend the money. Depreciation is a deduction for the expected <u>future</u> loss of the structure. For instance, if you buy a $50,000

An Intelligent Approach To Buying Real Estate

house, this price includes that land that it sits on and you are allowed, it's actually mandatory, to deduct the value of the structures depreciated over 27 1/2 years.

If we estimate the land value to be 10 percent of the purchase price, in this case $50,000, (the IRS would like for you to take 25 percent but I actually only take 5 percent for the land value (this is for my properties in Arizona, they may have a harder time agreeing with 5 percent in all states, see your accountant) but for this example we'll take 10 percent or $5,000), that would leave a depreciable value of $45,000. This deductible amount evenly distributed over 27 1/2 years would be $1,636 a year in deductions that you don't have to spend your hard earned money to get. So even if you break even with the rent compared to the mortgage payment and expenses, you would still get a $1,636 yearly deduction. If you are only in a 25 percent tax bracket, that amounts to over $400 per year lower tax burden that costs you nothing.

This coupled with all the other legal deductions that you'll be able to take, your tax burden will be decreased considerably. However, before investing in anything always talk with a good tax specialist first. If you don't have one, ask some of your friends if they use someone that they would recommend. Most friends won't recommend someone that isn't performing well for them. Don't even think of going to a nationally publicized company. You want to go to someone local, reliable and stable. You are going to need their services for years to come. Depreciation needs to be kept track of year after year. If you should need to find a new accountant some time in the future your previous tax returns will be able to help him to determine where you are with the depreciation.

George A. Cave

Some other items may need to be depreciated as well. These items are major dollar items like a new roof, carpet, appliances, air conditioners, etc. Each of these items have a different depreciation schedule. For instance a new roof may depreciate over ten years but carpet only three years. I don't depreciate appliances even though the IRS would like for me to. As I said earlier, in four audits they never made me change my return.

I have a policy with my rentals which is that if something costs less than $600 I take the deduction in the year of the expense and do not depreciate the item. (The IRS likes the figure of $300 but they still accepted my return "as is") So you can see why I wouldn't depreciate appliances in that I would never spend that much on a rental units appliance. My experience with the IRS is that if you have a policy, and the policy is reasonable, and you adhere to it, they are alright with it. I don't know what their billion page rule book says but after four audits they had no problem with the way I decide what to depreciate or not. Again, check with your accountant before making any assumptions.

I also take a certain amount of money each day that I am traveling or working on my properties for meals. The IRS has a per diem rate of $39 a day. I take $8 for breakfast, $12 for lunch and $19 for dinner, for a total of $39 a day. This way I don't have to keep a bunch of receipts. If you buy meals for other people, an entertainment expense, then you must have receipts. If I only work a half day at a property then I might just take the breakfast and lunch expense for a combined total of $20. If I leave for Arizona in mid-morning then I would take the lunch and dinner expense or $31. It makes life much

An Intelligent Approach To Buying Real Estate

easier than keeping all of those receipts. You certainly could keep the receipts if it makes you feel better or if your deduction would be higher.

I am not the one who dreamed up this plan. The company that I used to work for, yes I got free from that boss that I couldn't stand, did it this way and I figured that if it was alright for a multi-billion dollar company, then it was alright for me. The IRS didn't argue the point. The company that I used to work for did meal expenses the exact same way as I do. The amount set for their depreciable items was $2,500. I felt that $600 was reasonable with the type of investing that I do. This $600 amount is the same amount I use on my exotic bird breeding business and the IRS has no problem using that amount in that business either. In regards to real estate, even the $600 figure is not set in concrete. If it's a repair it can be entirely taken in the year that the money was spent. For instance, if you paint the house, that would be construed as a repair. If it cost $1,500, you can take the entire expense in that year.

I also take mileage rather than deducting the car payment, insurance, gas etc.. I drive about 30,000 miles a year and the IRS allows a thirty-one cent per mile deduction. In my case that amounts to a $9,300 deduction, much more than if I depreciated the car and deducted the insurance, repairs and gas. I also very rarely keep track of my mileage except for when I make a long trip. If I drive to Phoenix I reset the tripmeter on my car and record the miles once I get back home. If I'm driving around town I don't keep the mileage but have written down in a log how many miles it is to the places where I buy things. For instance, I know it's eight miles round trip to

George A. Cave

Home Depot and that's what my log states. When I buy something at Home Depot, for my rentals, I annotate that on the receipt along with which property it was for and log it into a ledger. Each property has its own ledger. I have a column in the ledger for the mileage that each trip required. At the end of the year I add them all up and that's the mileage. Easy.

I buy my record keeping ledgers at a local stationery store, a simple 12 column, green ledger and I put headings in each column. These columns include rent received, repairs, method of payment (cash, check, along with the check number, or credit card with the last four digits of the card being annotated for easy in finding the bill if necessary), appliances, utilities, air conditioning repairs, pest control, office supplies, replacement (depreciable items like carpet and roof), mileage and travel. I find this to be every bit as easy as logging it into a computer data base.

"The IRS Does Not Nit-pick"

My record keeping has become very good since the first audit. Before that it was somewhat lackadaisical. I remember the day that I got that ever famous letter from the IRS saying that they wanted to audit my taxes. I panicked. I immediately called my accountant and he recommended a service that specializes in tax audits. Big mistake. He was about as sloppy as he could be. I ended up going to the audit myself.

I went back over every receipt, every expenditure, every item I could find, and lo and behold I found more deductions than I had taken on my return. I went to the audit with a box full of files. The auditor was very thorough and went over

An Intelligent Approach To Buying Real Estate

every deduction over $200 on every house. This was the second bit of free information that the auditor gave me. The first bit of information was the reason why I was being audited. The reason was that I had a regular job, I filed a schedule E (real estate owned schedule) and a schedule C (personal business, bird breeder).

I had taken a loss on both the real estate, thank God for depreciation (when I started to invest in real estate, there was this thing called 'accelerated depreciation' which gave me much more depreciable write-off's over eighteen years instead of the current 27 1/2 years) and a loss on my exotic bird breeding business. Evidently this sends up several flags on their computer. This was the first year I claimed deductions for my bird breeding business. I know others that have had real estate for years and they have never been audited.

"Attitude Is Very Important"

The auditor agreed with all of my deductions and with all of my policies, meals and depreciation of the structures minus the land value, which I had placed at five percent of the purchase price. She also gave me some hints for how to help the audit go well in the event I was ever audited again. The first one was to be on time and don't miss the scheduled appointment date and be prompt to the appointment. You're the one who makes the appointment so keep it. Attitude is also very important. Mine was good so we didn't have any problems and she was very agreeable saying that she didn't want to discuss anything that was within $200 of the stated

George A. Cave

deduction or income. This was another great tidbit of information, the IRS does not nit-pick.

The audits were conducted in cubicles with walls only five feet high and I could hear the audit in the cubicle next to ours. This guy was not having a good day. He had no receipts, no canceled checks, no invoices, no nothing and the IRS figured he owed them about $20,000. He was really irate and was saying that his partner had run off with all the supporting documents. The auditor never got upset, and talked to him calmly the entire time but after a while said to the man in the hot seat "It appears that we are having some sort of a personality conflict, I don't know why but this is just not working out. Maybe it would be best if you spoke with someone else". That someone else turned out to be the auditor's supervisor. They went through the entire exercise again and at what was soon to be the conclusion of the audit, the supervisor told the auditee that if he didn't settle down and be cooperative very soon that his case would be kicked upstairs.

With that I couldn't stand it any longer and whispered to my auditor, "What does kick it upstairs mean"? She, very quietly replied, "That's not good, his audit is over, and it goes to court". Audit complete.

My next year's taxes were audited as well and by the same auditor, again with no additional taxes being levied. The following year was audited as well. By now I had my book keeping down to a science and it was merely a matter of picking up my ledgers and files and going down to the office.

An Intelligent Approach To Buying Real Estate

That year I had a different auditor and again there were no deductions that were not allowed on my real estate. However, my bird breeding business was a different story.

I'm including this story even though it doesn't pertain to real estate, because it does tell a very interesting story that may help those who get audited.

My deductions for my bird breeding business were in perfect shape but the auditor decided that the business was not a profit motivated business and therefore was going to disallow all of the deductions for that business. (This type of problem will probably never happen with real estate investing.) I explained to her that it was a profit motivated business but there was no moving her. The IRS rule book says that in order to take a deduction for a business that business must have a motive to make a profit. What the auditor was saying was that my bird breeding business was a hobby.

She said that she would think about my explanation a little more and send me a letter as to her final decision. A few weeks later I got the answer. Surprise, it was not in my favor. The IRS was asking me to pay $2,500 in additional taxes, plus interest and penalties, because the auditor could not see how I was ever going to be able to turn a profit on my bird breeding business. Even though I explained to her that the audit was being done on a four year old tax return and next year I would be making a profit. She didn't buy it. (This is where most people just give up and send the IRS whatever the amount is that they ask for. The IRS can be very intimidating and most people don't wish to irritate them. I knew that I was right and I was not going to give in just because an auditor couldn't fathom how I was going to make money at my business.)

George A. Cave

When the letter arrived it came with a form letter in the event that I wanted to disagree with the auditor's findings and appeal the case, which of course I did. Several months later I got a letter with an appointment date and time to go back to the IRS for the appeal. When I went to the appeal appointment, guess what, the same auditor was doing the appeal. She once again said that she could not see how I was ever going to make a profit and she was going to disallow the expenses. I told her that it was not my responsibility to educate the IRS on bird breeding nor was it up to her to determine what kind of business I could deduct expenses on. My business was profit motivated and I felt that any judge in a court of law, even a tax court, would be able to see that.

She then asked me if I wanted to appeal further. I told her that we might as well go straight to court because I have no intention of paying any additional taxes. So we filled out the paperwork right there in her office. Again I must stress not to lose your temper, even though it was very difficult to do at this point. The auditors are just doing their job, as distasteful as it may be, and that job is to collect money for the government.

As I was waiting for the paperwork to come back for going to court I got another audit letter for the next year's taxes. I showed up for my appointment and it was the same auditor that would not allow my bird business expenses. This was a very quick audit. She only wanted to see the bird business ledger and as usual everything was in order and again she was going to disallow the expenses because she still didn't feel that it was a profit motivated business. I suggested that we go straight to court with this year as well and have both years heard at the same time. She agreed.

An Intelligent Approach To Buying Real Estate

A couple of months went by before I got the paperwork for tax court. The forms are very easy to understand and I filled them out myself and sent them in. A short time after sending in this paperwork I got a letter from a branch of the IRS that tries to arbitrate cases before they go to court.

I called the number on the form and spoke to the person that was handling my case. She explained that her department was an unbiased third party and, if I was willing, she would sit down with me and go over my case impartially and see if we couldn't resolve this matter without going to court.

I made an appointment and showed up with all of my receipts and ledger. The arbitrator was very friendly and patiently listened to all of the reasons why I knew that my business was profit motivated. She explained that a business should make a profit two out of five years to be a profit motivated business and I had taken a loss for five consecutive years. (This rule does not apply to real estate. You can take a loss every year, forever.)

I went on to explain that in order to start my business up properly it would take approximately $100,000. Since I didn't have that kind of money to start the business all at once it was done over a course of several years and my understanding of the profit motivated rule was that I had to be moving in a positive direction with profit in mind. I went on to explain that, as I understood it, the two out of five year rule was more of a guideline than a rule.

The arbitrator showed me some case findings of unsuccessful pet shops that were deemed not-for-profit having lost money year after year. The IRS claimed the losses were not allowed because the owner didn't have the proper

George A. Cave

knowledge to run a pet shop and didn't do anything to get himself educated and therefore the IRS disallowed the expense and it was held up in court. I didn't feel that these cases applied to my situation and told the arbitrator so.

I explained to the arbitrator that at this particular point in time I had quit my 9 to 5 job and was indeed living off of the profit from my bird collection and other investments and that we were talking about an audit of a five year old tax return. She told me that it was obvious to her that the government had no case in regards to the not for profit motivation. She went on to say that she had reviewed my tax return prior to our meeting and she saw some deductions that could be construed as personal and not business related. I explained that my return had already been audited and there were no problems with any of the deductions. The only problem was whether or not it was profit motivated. She told me that she wanted me to go home and write down answers to the questions that she had on a type of checklist to help determine if a business was profit motivated or not, and to review my deductions to see if any of them could be construed as personal, whether they were or not, and to think about an amount that I would be willing to pay to settle this action without going to court.

I took the list home and answered the questions in depth. I didn't finish the written response for about two months since I was in no hurry and talking to the arbitrator was strictly voluntary. I didn't feel that the arbitrator was sincere in her unbiased third party role in that the first word out of her mouth was settlement. These were also the last words from her. I was feeling more and more confident that I was going to be going to court.

An Intelligent Approach To Buying Real Estate

Finally the letter arrived that told me that my court date was in 30 days. I got a call the next day from the arbitrator who wanted to go over my case again with an amount that she felt was fair. She wanted me to pay $900 plus interest for five years plus late charges. That would bring the balance to about $1,600 instead of the nearly $3,200 that the IRS was now asking for.

I told the arbitrator that she said herself that the government had no case against me in regards to the not-for-profit claim and that was the only thing that the court was to decide. She said that was true but there were some deductions that appeared to be personal and she deducted these items and came up with the $900. She then asked me if I understood what her role was. I explained that I thought that I had, but now I can see that her job is not an unbiased third party but a last chance effort by the IRS to extort money from a citizen that clearly doesn't owe them anything. (But I said it in a really nice tone of voice.)

At that she got really upset saying "I've bent over backwards to help you in this case and you accuse me of trying to extort money from you? This is the thanks I get for trying to help you out"?

I very calmly replied, "How is asking me to pay $900 that I don't owe, helping me out? The issue is whether or not my business is profit motivated and I believe that the judge will see that it is since it is currently my main source of income. I have also received the decision on the following year's appeal for the same issue and it came back approved as submitted. So the IRS themselves dropped the claim in the next year's tax return".

George A. Cave

Still irate she said "If you go to court the amount the judge will be looking at will be the original $2,500, it will not be the $900, you have to agree to this right now or I will withdraw the offer".

I suggested that I could come into her office and explain any of the items that she felt could have been construed as personal and she would see that I didn't owe anything. I went on to tell her that it was my understanding that the only issue the judge would be deciding was the profit motivation issue and that I felt very comfortable that he would see things my way.

She started to settle down and asked me when could I come in and go over the expenses with her. I told her at her earliest convenience. We scheduled an appointment for the following week. I felt that I had nothing to lose by going to court but also was willing to settle it without going if at all possible.

The next day I got a message on my answering machine from the arbitrator saying "Mr. Cave, I spoke with my supervisor about your case and she agreed that the government has no legitimate claim against you. It appears that the way the original auditor wrote up the case, the only issue is whether or not your business is profit motivated. I would have done it differently but the way it currently is, the government has no case against you. Please call as soon as you can and if it's alright with you the government will enter a stipulation to the court dropping the claim".

I called her back just as soon as I could and once again she was as nice as could be, seemingly forgetting that just yesterday she tried to get me to pay $1,600 in taxes, interest

An Intelligent Approach To Buying Real Estate

and fines that I didn't owe, and got upset when I didn't just roll over and play dead and pay it. I, of course, continued to keep my composure and agreed to sign the necessary paperwork so as not to go to court. Case Closed.

If you read between the lines in this case you will see that it makes a great deal of sense, even if you do owe them money, getting to this arbitration stage. Even if my business had not been profit motivated, I could have settled the case for less than half of what they were originally asking for. I have a friend that is very aggressive in his tax deductions and is audited almost every year, and every year they disallow several expenses that very often amount to over $5,000 in additional taxes owed. He fights them every time and every time he takes it to the point where they are willing to settle on a lesser amount and that's what he pays. He claims that he saves a fortune on his income taxes this way.

I am not suggesting that you file an untrue tax return in an attempt to keep from paying your share of the tax burden in this country. However, the government decides the rules of exemptions and deductions and even though I am a firm believer in "giving to Caesar that which belongs to him", I also will use every legal means available to keep that amount as low as possible.

The moral of the story is don't be afraid of the IRS, they are not unreasonable most of the time. Real Estate is probably one of the least audited items in that it's so easy to prove your deductions. The government also feels that we landlords are doing the country a service by providing housing to people who cannot afford to purchase their own. Keep good records

George A. Cave

and take all of your legitimate deductions, and talk to a good tax accountant prior to making <u>any</u> investments.

Glossary of Terms, Examples and Insights

Absolute Fee Simple Title: Absolute or fee-simple title is one that is absolute and unqualified. It is the best title one can have.

Abstract of Judgment: A condensation of the essential provisions of a court judgment.

Abstract of Title: Summary of digest of documents affecting title to real estate.

Abstraction: A method of valuing land. The indicated value of the improvement is deducted from the sale price.

Abutting: Land that borders or touches the land of others. This would be your property line.

George A. Cave

Acceleration Clause: Provision in a trust deed or mortgage which causes the balance owed to be immediately due and payable upon a particular happening of a certain event. The acceleration clause is often used in the event of an unassumable loan that changes title. In this case the lender calls the loan to be all due and payable or they foreclose on the property.

Acceptance: When the seller or agent's principal agrees to the terms of the agreement of sale and approves the negotiation on the part of the agent and acknowledges receipt of the deposit in subscribing to the agreement of sale, that act is termed an acceptance.

Access Right: The right of an owner to have ingress and egress to and from his property, also called right of way.

Accrued Depreciation: Depreciation which has accumulated over a period of time.

Accrued Items of Expense: Those incurred expenses which are not yet payable. the seller's accrued expenses are credited to the purchaser in a closing statement.

Acknowledgment: A formal declaration before a notary public or other authorized official by a person who has executed a document, that he in fact did execute (sign) the document.

An Intelligent Approach to Buying Real Estate

Acquisition: The act or process by which a person procures property.

Acre: A unit of measured land equaling 43,560 square feet or 209' by 209'.

Actuary: A person professionally trained in the technical aspects of insurance, particularly in the mathematics of mortality tables and the calculation of premiums, reserves and other values.

Adjusted Cost Basis: The value of property shown on the books of a taxpayer. The formula is: original cost plus improvements less accumulated cost recovery deductions equals adjusted cost basis.

Adjustments: A means by which characteristics of a residential property are regulated by dollar amount or percentage to conform to similar characteristics of another residential property.

Adjustable Rate Mortgage: A mortgage, real estate loan, with an interest rate that will be changed from time to time, usually at predetermined intervals, based on the changes of a specified index. (See index, spread, cap)

Administrator: A person appointed by the probate court to administer to estate of a person deceased.

George A. Cave

Ad Valorem: A Latin term meaning "to value" or "in proportion to the value".

Advance: Transfer of funds from a lender to a borrower in advance on a loan.

Advance Commitment: The institutional investor's prior agreement to provide long-term financing upon completion of construction.

Advance Fee: A fee paid in advance of <u>any</u> services rendered. Specifically that unethical practice of obtaining a fee in advance for the advertising of property or businesses for sale, with no obligation to obtain a buyer, by persons representing themselves as real estate licensees, or representatives of licensed real estate firms.

Adverse Possession: The open and notorious possession and occupancy under an evident claim or right, in denial or opposition to the title of another claimant.

Affidavit: A written statement of facts sworn to or affirmed by oath before a notary public or other authorized official.

Agency: The relationship between principal and agent which arises out of a contract, either expressed or implied, written or oral, wherein the agent is employed by the principal to perform certain acts dealing with a third party.

An Intelligent Approach to Buying Real Estate

Agent: One who represents another from whom he or she has derived authority.

Agreement of Sale: A written agreement or contract between seller and purchaser in which they reach a meeting of minds on the terms and conditions of the sale.

Air Rights: The rights in real property to use the air space above the surface of the land.

Alienate: To transfer the title to real property from one person to another.

A.L.T.A. Title Policy: (American Land Title Association) An expanded coverage title insurance policy issued to lenders

Amenities: Features of a piece of property that make it attractive and/or desirable. Amenities are light fixtures, floor coverings, skylights etc., nearly anything but the structure itself. Amenities may also include the property's proximity to schools and shopping.

Amenity Value: A subjective or perceived amount given in dollars, for the value of certain amenities such as good neighborhood, schools, parks, playgrounds, etc.

Amortization: A schedule to pay off a debt in regular installments, usually monthly, with the principal balance being reduced to a point of complete payoff of the debt or mortgage.

George A. Cave

Amortized loan: A loan where the principal payments are to be paid in certain, usually equal installments until the loan is completely paid off. For instance a $100,000 loan fully amortized over 30 years at a fixed interest rate of 8% would have a monthly payment of $733.77 (principal and interest only). At the end of the term of 30 years the loan would be paid in full. Also called a "level payment plan".

Annuity: A series of assured equal or nearly equal payments to be made over a period of time or it may be a lump-sum payment to be made in the future. The installment payments due to the landlord under a lease is an annuity. So are the installment payments due to a lender. In real estate finance we are most concerned with the first definition.

Appraisal: The reasonable value attached to a specific piece of property by the opinion of the appraiser. There are several ways of appraising a property. The most popular method is the **'Comparative Analysis'** where comparable homes in the area that have sold recently are compared to the subject property and based on their selling price a fair value is assign to the subject property. Another method of appraisal is the **'Income or Capitalization Method'**, where a value is assigned by means of a property's income generating potential. For instance, if a four-plex collects rents in the amount of $500 each for a total of $2,000 a month and the expenses to run the property (not including the mortgage) are $300 a month, the gross rent is $1,700 a month. A specific multiplying factor is assigned, in this case times ten, the property would then be worth $170,000. The multiplying factor is somewhat arbitrary

An Intelligent Approach to Buying Real Estate

and other factors need to be taken into account such as the condition of the building, the location, etc. Still another method of appraisal is the **'Cost Approach'** method where the cost of replacing the structure is determined and then money is deducted for depreciation and necessary repairs.

Appraiser: A person qualified by education, training and experience, who is hired to estimate the value of real and personal property based on experience, judgment, facts and use of formal appraisal processes.

Appreciation: The increase in value of a property, for any reason.

Appurtenance: Anything that is part of the property or to the land, such as a house, driveway, fence, etc.

Assessed Value: Value placed on property as a basis for taxation.

Assessment: The valuation of property for the purpose of levying a tax or the amount of the tax levied.

Assessor: The official who has the responsibility of determining assessed values. Usually a government official.

Assign: To transfer to another a claim, a right, or a title to property.

Assignee: The person to whom property is transferred.

George A. Cave

Assignment: The legal transfer of rights or interests in property to another person.

Assignments of Rents Clause: A clause in a trust deed which, in the event of a default, gives the beneficiary the right to collect rents of the secured property.

Assumption: The act of assuming or taking over the primary responsibility for payment of an existing mortgage or trust deed.

Assumption Fee: A lender's charge for changing over and processing new records for a new owner who is assuming an existing loan.

Assets: Something of value, including but not limited to, cash, investments, real estate, personal property, trust deeds held, etc.

Attachment: Seizure of property by court order, usually done to have it available in event a judgment is obtained against the property or property holder in a pending suit.

Attest: To affirm to be true or genuine; an official act establishing authenticity.

Attorney In Fact: One who is authorized to perform certain acts for another under a power of attorney; power of attorney may be limited to a specific act or acts, or be valid in general.

An Intelligent Approach to Buying Real Estate

Balance Sheet: A financial statement which, as of a specific date, shows asset, liabilities and net worth.

Balloon Payment: The final payment on a note which is greater than the preceding installment payments. The Real Estate Law considers that any final payment twice as great as the smallest installment payment to be a balloon payment.

Basis: For income tax purposes, basis is property's original cost plus capital improvements and less accumulated cost recovery deduction. Also referred to as "book value".

Bearing Wall or Partition: A wall or partition supporting any vertical load in addition to its own weight.

Beneficiary: One (lender) who receives the income from a Trustor(borrower). The lender on a note and trust deed transaction. Also a person named in an insurance policy or a will to receive property.

Beneficiary's Statement: Statement of a lender (beneficiary), usually obtained when an owner wishes to sell or refinance, giving the remaining principal balance and other information concerning the loan. Also referred to as a "Bene Statement" or "Offset Statement".

Bequest: That which is given by the terms of a will.

Betterment: An improvement upon property which increases the property value and is considered as a capital asset as distinguished from repairs or replacements where the original character or cost is unchanged.

Bill of Sale: A document used to transfer the title or ownership of personal property.

Binder: An agreement to consider a down payment for the purchase of real estate as evidence of good faith on the part of the purchaser. Also, a notation of coverage on an insurance policy, issued by an agent, and given to the insured prior to issuing of the policy.

Blanket Mortgage (or Trust Deed): A mortgage or trust deed which covers more than one lot or parcel of real estate.

Blighted Area: A declining area in which real property values are seriously affected by destructive economic forces, such as encroaching inharmonious property usage's, infiltration of lower social and economic classes of inhabitants, and/or rapidly depreciating structures.

Bona Fide: In good faith, without fraud.

Bond: An obligation under seal. A real estate bond is a written obligation issued on the security of a mortgage or trust deed.

An Intelligent Approach to Buying Real Estate

Breach: The breaking of a law, or failure of duty, either by omission or commission.

Broker: A person who acts in the interest of another with the expectation of being compensated for his efforts in real estate, insurance, securities or related transactions. In real estate the Broker must be licensed. Realtors, real estate agents, generally work for a Broker.

Broker's Loan Statement: A written statement signed and received by the borrower at the time of a loan transaction, indicating the maximum cost, expenses, commissions, etc., to be paid by the borrower of a loan.

B. T. U.: British thermal unit. The quantity of heat required to raise the temperature of one pound of water one degree Fahrenheit.

Building Code: a state, city or county law which sets forth minimum building construction standards.

Building Residual Technique: One of the methods of appraising a building, or determining it's accrued depreciation.

Built-ins: Cabinets or similar features built as part of the house.

Bundle of Rights: Beneficial interests or rights.

Cap: The maximum amount, in percent, that an adjustable rate mortgage can rise. For instance an ARM with an initial rate of 6% with a 5 point cap, can never reach an interest rate higher than 11%. (see Adjustable Rate Mortgage, Index, Spread)

Capital Assets: Assets of a permanent nature used in the production of an income, such as: land, buildings, machinery, and equipment. Under income tax law, it is usually distinguishable from "inventory" which comprises assets held for sale to customers in the ordinary course of the taxpayer's trade or business.

Capital Gain or Capital Loss: Profit or loss from the sale of a capital asset. A capital gain, under federal income tax laws, may be either short term (12 months or less) or long term (longer than 12 months). A short term capital gain is taxed at the reporting individual's full income tax rate. A long term capital gain is taxed at a maximum of 28 percent; the actual tax rate depends upon the reporting individual's tax bracket.

Any capital gain is taken in the year of the gain. In the event of a loss, that loss is also taken in the year of the sale of the asset.

In the event of a property being sold with a capital gain but some of that gain is in the form of a trust deed, owner carryback. The taxpayer has the choice to take the payment paid yearly on the carryback as income as they are made or to take the entire gain in the year of that gain. Naturally, any cash that the seller realized falls under the normal capital gains law and must be declared in the year received.

An Intelligent Approach to Buying Real Estate

Capitalization: With respect to appraising, determining value of property by considering net income and percentage of reasonable return on the investment. Thus, the value of an income property is determined by dividing annual net income by the capitalization rate.

Capitalization Rate: The rate of interest which is considered a reasonable return on the investment, and used in the process of determining value based upon net income. It may also be described as the yield rate that is necessary to attract the money of the average investor to a particular kind of investment.

Cash Flow: The net income, or spendable income from an investment after deducting the costs of maintaining the investment, including the mortgage payment, taxes, insurance, repairs, management, and any other expense incurred by the investment as compared to the income generated by the investment.

Caveat Emptor: "Let the buyer beware". The buyer must examine the goods or property and buy at his or her own risk. Take nothing for granted. There are unscrupulous sellers, buyers and agents out there. If a deal sounds too good to be true it probably is.

Certificate of Reasonable Value: The Veterans Administration appraisal commitment of property value. One of the two documents needed by a veteran to secure a VA loan. The other document being the "Certificate of Entitlement". (These two documents are not necessary when purchasing VA foreclosures from the Veterans Administration.)

Certificate of Taxes Due: A written statement or guaranty of the condition of the taxes on a certain property, made by the county treasurer of the county wherein the property is located. Any loss resulting to any person from an error in a tax certificate shall be paid by the county which such treasurer represents.

Certificate of Title: A statement furnished by an abstract company to its customer which states that, based upon its records, title is properly vested in the present owner.

Chain of Title: A listing, chronologically, of all of the documents transferring title to a parcel of real estate, beginning with the document originally transferring title from the government to private ownership and ending with the latest document transferring title.

Chattel Mortgage: A personal property mortgage.

Class: The statutory percentage applicable to an asset depends upon the property's class.

Closing Costs: The costs associated with the escrow of the sale of property. Closing costs include but are not limited to: appraisal fee, escrow fees, title insurance fee, tax fees,

An Intelligent Approach to Buying Real Estate

Prorations of interest, taxes and insurance, document fees, filing fees, and a host of others. Fees vary greatly from state to state.

Closing Statement: A financial statement rendered to the buyer and seller at the close of escrow, giving an account of all funds received or expended by the escrow holder. Required by law to be made at the completion of every real estate transaction done through an escrow company.

Cloud On The Title: Any condition which affects the clear title to real property; usually relatively unimportant items but which cannot be removed without a quitclaim deed or court action.

Collateral: This is the property subject to the security interest.

Collateral Security: A separate obligation attached to a contract to guarantee its performance; the transfer of property or of other contracts, or valuables, to insure the performance of a principal agreement.

Collusion: An agreement between two or more persons to defraud another's right by the forms of law, or to obtain an object forbidden by law.

Color of Title: That which appears to be good title but which is not title in fact.

George A. Cave

Commercial Acre: A term applied to the remainder of an acre of newly subdivided land after the area devoted to streets, sidewalks and curbs, and so on, has been deducted from the acre.

Commission: An agent's compensation for performing agency duties; in real estate practice, a percentage of the selling price of property, percentage of rentals, and so forth.

Commitment: A pledge or a promise or firm agreement. A agreement to loan money.

Common Law: The body of law that grew from customs and practices developed and used in England "since the memory of man runneth not to the contrary".

Comparative Analysis: A method of appraising property where the selling prices of similar properties are compared to the property being appraised. Also known as the Market Data Approach.

Community: A part of a metropolitan area that has a number of neighborhoods that have a tendency toward common interests and problems.

Community Property: Property accumulated through joint efforts of a married couple.

An Intelligent Approach to Buying Real Estate

Comparable Sales: sales which have similar characteristics as the subject property and are used for analysis in the appraisal process.

Competent: Legally qualified

Compound Interest: Interest paid on original principal and also on the accrued and unpaid interest that has accumulated.

Conclusion: The final estimate of value, realized from the facts, data, experience and judgment.

Condemnation: 1) An act by the government of appropriating private property (through the exercise of the power of eminent domain) for public use upon the payment of fair compensation. 2) The declaration that a structure is unfit for use.

Condition: A stipulation or qualification in a deed, which if violated or not performed, defeats the deed and places the title back in the hands of the original grantor. Also may be a requirement that must be met before the performance or completion of the contract.

Condition Precedent: A condition that requires certain action or the happening of a specified event before the estate granted can take effect. An example would be that most installment real estate sale contracts state all payments shall be made at the time specified before the buyer may demand transfer of title.

George A. Cave

Conditional Sales Contract: A contract for the sale of real or personal property in which possession is delivered to the buyer, title to remain vested in the seller until all the conditions of the contract have been fulfilled. Title of the property sold does not go to the buyer until the loan is paid off. This type of sales contract, in most states, is the easiest to foreclose on because title of the property never changed. Also called a "Land Contract".

Condition Subsequent: When there is a condition subsequent in a deed, the title vests immediately in the grantee, but upon breach of the condition the grantor has the power to terminate the estate. For example, a condition in the deed prohibiting the grantee from using the premises as a liquor store.

Conditional Commitment: A commitment of a definite loan amount for some future unknown purchaser of satisfactory credit standing.

Condominium: A residential building consisting of multiple units, individually owned. Real property where the owner has an undivided interest in common with respect to the land and outside of the buildings. The individual owner usually owns the interior of the structure while the exterior of the buildings along with the land and other amenities such as pools, tennis courts, parking lots, etc. are all held in common with the other owners.

Condominiums are great for investors because there is no exterior maintenance. They are generally less expensive to buy than single family homes and the rents are usually comparable

An Intelligent Approach to Buying Real Estate

to single family homes. There is, however, a homeowners association fee assessed monthly. Before buying into any condominium complex, verify the abilities of the homeowners Board of Directors to manage to finances of the complex professionally and competently. Many condominium complexes end up with very high monthly dues because the elected Board of Directors are not properly equipped to manage the complex.

Confession of Judgment: An entry of judgment upon the debtor's voluntary admission or confession.

Confirmation of Sale: A court approval of the sale of property by an executor, administrator, guardian or conservator.

Confiscation: The seizing of property without compensation.

Consideration: Anything of value to induce another to enter into a contract. May be money, services, a promise, or love and affection. Sometimes stated as "For valuable consideration..."

Constant: The percentage which, when applied directly to the face value of a debt, develops the annual amount of money necessary to pay a specified net rate of interest on the reducing balance and to liquidate the debt in a specified time period. For instance, a 6% loan with a 20 year amortization has a constant of approximately 8 1/2%. Thus, a $10,000 loan amortized over 20 years requires an annual payment of approximately $850. (An annual payment of $850 is 8 1/2% of the loan amount, $10,000)

Construction Loans: Loans made for the construction of homes or commercial buildings. Usually funds are disbursed to the contractor-builder during construction and after periodic inspections. Disbursements are based on an agreement between borrower and lender.

Constructive Eviction: Breach of a covenant of warranty or quiet enjoyment, e.g., the inability of a lessee to obtain possession because of a paramount defect in title, or a condition making occupancy hazardous. For example, the house is condemned or unsafe for inhabitation.

Constructive Notice: Notice given by the public records.

Consummate Dower: A widow's dower interest which, after the death of her husband, is complete or may be completed and become an interest in real estate.

Contiguous: Adjoining or touching upon, such as parcels of land next to each other.

Contingency: A specific condition upon which a valid contract is dependent.

Contract: A mutual agreement by two or more parties to do or not to do a certain thing. Oral or written.

An Intelligent Approach to Buying Real Estate

Conventional Financing: Any loan made without government participation.

Conversion: Change from one character or use to another.

Convey: To transfer title of property from one person to another. To assign title to another.

Conveyance: A document, such as a deed, used to transfer title to property from one person to another.

Cooperative Ownership: A form of apartment ownership. Ownership of shares in a cooperative venture which entitles the owner to use, rent or sell a specific apartment unit. The corporation usually reserves the right to approve certain actions such as a sale or improvement.

Corporation: An artificial or legal "person" (entity), created by laws, which has many of the powers and duties of an individual. A corporation is a creature of law having certain powers and duties of a natural person. Being created by law it may continue for any length of time the law prescribes.

Corporeal Rights: Possessor's rights in real estate.

Cost Approach: An appraisal technique used to establish value of property by estimating the cost to reproduce the improvements, allowing for depreciation and adding the market value of the land.

George A. Cave

Covenant: A clause in a contract; a promise; an agreement contained in a deed to require or prohibit performance of certain acts, or to restrict the use or non-use of the property.

Creditor: One to whom a debt is owed. Opposite of Debtor.

Curable Depreciation: Items of physical deterioration and functional obsolescence which are customarily repaired or replaced by a prudent property owner.

Curtail Schedule: A listing of the amounts by which the principal sum of an obligation is to be reduced by partial payments and of the dates when each payment will become payable.

Curtesy: The rights which a husband has in a wife's estate at her death.

Damages: Money payment ordered by a court to be paid to one whose property rights or personal rights have been violated.

Debenture: Bonds issued without security.

Debtor: One who owes a debt. Anyone liable for a claim.

Deck: Usually an open porch on the roof of a ground or lower floor, porch or wing.

An Intelligent Approach to Buying Real Estate

Declaration of Abandonment: Document that must be recorded to terminate a homestead.

Decree: A specific type of court order.

Decree of Foreclosure: Decree by a court in the completion of foreclosure of a mortgage, contract, or lien.

Dedication: An appropriation of land by its owner for some public use accepted for such use by authorized public officials on behalf of the public.

Deed: A written instrument which, when properly executed and delivered, transfers title of real estate.

Deed of Reconveyance: The transfer of legal title from the trustee (lien holder) to the trust (borrower) after a trust deed debt has been paid.

Deed Restrictions: This is a limitation in the deed to a property that dictates certain uses that may or may not be made of the property.

Default: Failure to fulfill a legal duty or obligation pertaining to a legal contract. Not making the payments on a mortgage will, upon written notice from the lender, put a property into default. This is generally the first stage of a foreclosure and is a legal procedure. This procedure can generally be stopped by making up the missed payments and paying the late fees and any accumulated charges, depending upon the terms and conditions set forth in the contract.

Default Judgment: A court order resulting from the failure of a defendant to answer a complaint in a lawsuit.

Defeasible: Ownership but with conditional restrictions which, if not obeyed, can result in forfeiture of the title to the grantor or his heirs.

Deferred Maintenance: Existing but unfulfilled requirement for repairs and rehabilitation.

Deferred Payment Options: The privilege of deferring income payments to take advantage of the tax statutes.

Deficiency Judgment: A judgment given when the security pledge for a loan does not satisfy the debt upon its default.

Demise: A transfer to another of an estate for years, for life, or at will.

Deposit Receipt: A receipt acknowledging the acceptance of "earnest money" (deposit) to bind an offer to purchase real property. When a contract is signed by all parties there is generally a deposit made to show good faith on the side of the buyer. This deposit is not a legal requirement and is not legally necessary to purchase real estate.

An Intelligent Approach to Buying Real Estate

Depreciation: The loss in value due to any reason. Real depreciation is the actual loss in value due to age, neglect, market conditions or even normal wear and tear. Depreciation in the context of income taxes may be only a paper loss in that depreciation is deducted from a person's tax liability regardless whether or not the property has actually gone down in value or increased in value.

One of the greatest benefits of real estate investing is depreciation. The theory is that over a period of time the structure will become worthless. The beautiful thing about depreciation is that you don't have to spend money to get it, like you must do for all other deductions. The interest, taxes, repairs, etc. are all deductions _after_ you spend the money. Depreciation is a deduction for the expected _future_ loss of the structure.

For instance, if you buy a $50,000 house, this price includes the land that it sits on and you are allowed (actually it's mandatory) to deduct the value of the structures depreciated over 27 1/2 years. If we estimate the land value to be 10% of the purchase price, in this case $50,000, (the IRS would like for you to take 20% but I actually only take 5% for the land value but for this example we'll take 10% or $5,000), that would leave a depreciable value of $45,000. This deductible amount evenly distributed over 27 1/2 years would be $1,636 a year in deductions that you don't have to spend your hard earned money to get. So even if you break even with the rent compared to the mortgage payment and expenses, you would still get a $1,636 yearly deduction. If you are only in a 25% tax bracket that amounts to a $400 decrease in your tax burden.

George A. Cave

Desist and Refrain Order: An order directing a person to desist (to stop) and refrain from committing an act in violation of the real estate law.

Deterioration: Impairment of condition. One of the causes of depreciation and reflecting the loss in value brought about by wear and tear, disintegration, use in service, and the action of the elements.

Directional growth: The location or direction toward which the residential sections of a city are destined or determined to grow.

Discount: To sell a note for less than its face value. To receive the present value of a note minus a deduction to cover interest.

Discount Points. A loan fee that is charged by a lender when accepting FHA or G. I. Loans, to offset the lower interest received in comparison with conventions loan interest rates. Buyer, Seller, or broker may pay all or part. Government loans are currently open for negotiation with regards to the interest rate and whether it's a fixed, variable or graduated loan and discount points may no longer be applicable depending upon the loan program that you decide upon.

Disintermediation: The relatively sudden withdrawal of substantial sums of money savers have deposited with savings and loan associations, commercial banks, and mutual savings

An Intelligent Approach to Buying Real Estate

banks. This term can also be considered to include life insurance policy purchasers borrowing against the value of their policies. The essence of this phenomenon is financial intermediaries losing within a short period of time billions of dollars as owners of funds held by those institutional lenders exercise their prerogative of taking them out of the hands of these financial institutions.

Disposable Income: The after-tax income a household receives to spend on personal consumption.

Dispossess: To deprive one of the use of real estate

Distressed Seller: A seller that has to sell his property due to circumstances beyond his immediate control and is willing to do it even at a loss. A distressed seller might be a person who has lost his job, is going or has gone through a divorce, someone who may have gotten in over his head, financially, or has made to many bad investments. A distressed seller needs to sell his property very quickly.
    A distressed seller may also be someone that didn't turn out to be landlord material and just wants to get rid of the headache of being one.

Documentary Transfer Tax: A state enabling act, or law, allowing a county to adopt a documentary transfer tax to apply on all transfer of real property located in the county. Notice of payment is entered on face of the deed or on a separate paper filled with the deed.

George A. Cave

Donee: A person to whom a gift is made.

Donor: A person who makes a gift.

Dower: The right which a wife has in her husband's estate at his death. (also see Curtesy)

Earnest Money: Down payment made by a purchaser of real estate as evidence of good faith. Not a legal requirement.

Easement: A legal right granted to use the land of another, often for the purpose of utility lines, fences, driveways, etc.

Easement in Gross: An easement held by a public utility company which is not attached to any specific piece of land. This is a general easement, or right to pass, allowing utility companies, for example, to gain access to utility poles and lines regardless of whose land they may be on or pass over.

Economic Life: The period over which a property will yield a return on the investment, over and above the economic or ground rent due to land.

Economic Obsolescence: Loss in value of a piece of property due to the reduced desirability and usefulness of a structure, real or supposed, from extraneous causes such as the deterioration of a neighborhood or zoning regulations. Also referred to as Social Obsolescence.

An Intelligent Approach to Buying Real Estate

Economic Rent: The reasonable rental expectancy if the property were available for renting at the time of its valuation.

Effective Age: The age that an appraiser assigns to an improvement that reflects the true age of an improvement and not necessarily the actual chronological age of an improvement. For instance, a house may be 20 years old but has been maintained very well and so an appraiser may assign an 'effective age' of 17 years. The reverse would be true also in the case of a property that has not been kept up.

Effective Date of Value: The specific day the conclusion of value applies.

Eminent Domain: The power of the government, federal, state, or local, to take private property for a public use. The owner is compensated for his property but has no choice but to sell it for the good of the public use.

Encroachment: The building of a structure wholly or in part upon the land of another without any legal right to do so.

Encumber: To place a lien or charge on property.

Encumbrance: Anything which burdens (limits) the free title to property, such as a lien, an easement, or a restriction of any kind.

George A. Cave

Endorsement: That signature made on the reverse side of a promissory note or check for the purpose of transferring ownership.
"In Blank" - guarantees payment to subsequent holders.
"Without Recourse" - does not guarantee payment to subsequent holders.

Equity: The value of real estate above any liens that may be held against it. For instance if a property is worth $100,000 and the total indebtedness on the property is $65,000, the amount of equity is $35,000.

Equity of Redemption: That right of an owner, for one year, to redeem property following a mortgage foreclosure sale.

Escalation: The right reserved by the lender to increase the amount of the payments and/or interest upon the happening of a certain event. This is the case in variable rate mortgages.

Escheat: The reverting of property to the state when heirs capable of inheriting are lacking. This is a very good reason to have a will in place that dispositions your real estate in the event of your death.

Escrow: A transaction, usually a sale, wherein one person delivers evidence of title to a third person to be held by such third person until the happening of the performance of a prescribed condition, after which the evidence of title is then delivered to the buyer.

An Intelligent Approach to Buying Real Estate

Escrow Holder: A third party, usually a corporation, which acts as the agent for buyer and seller, protecting the interest of each.

Estate: As applied to the real estate practice, the term signifies the quantity of interest, share, right, equity, of which riches or fortune may consist, in real property. The degree, quantity, nature, and extent of interest which a person has in real property.

Estate of Inheritance: An estate which may descend to heirs. All freehold estates are estates of inheritance, except estates for life.

Estates for Life: A freehold estate, not of inheritance, but which is held by the tenant for his or her own life or the life or lives of one or more other persons, or for an indefinite period which may endure for the life or lives of persons in being and beyond the period of life.

Estate from Period to Period: An interest in land where there is no definite termination date but the rental period is fixed at a certain sum per week, month, or year. Also called a periodic tenancy.

Estate Planning: The process of long term planning for estate preservation. Estate planning may have many goals to be considered with only a few of them being, tax shelters, equity growth, cash flow, and retirement. Tax shelters may be real property that are at a break even cashflow and require very

George A. Cave

little of your time. Eventually these properties will be paid off or the loan value will become low enough to fall into one of the other categories.

Equity growth are properties that you buy at a discount because of their physical condition or that maybe were purchased through a foreclosure. When these properties are fixed up they are worth substantially more than they were when they were acquired. Turning these around for a quick profit would not be a bad plan and then go on to the next property.

Cash flow comes from income producing properties. These properties might have a low mortgage, may be owned free and clear and will produce a positive cash flow. These properties will eventually paid off and they will continue to produce even more cash flow.

Retirement is what estate planning is all about. That someday we will have the money to stop working for our money and let our money, or investments, work for us. Real estate is the perfect vehicle to accomplish this goal. With real estate, it can purchased with little or no money, paid off by the tenants over a long period of time and when it's paid off will provide for an excellent source of retirement income. Retirement could come much earlier than the standard 65 years, as soon as ones income is sufficient to support oneself, you can retire.

Estate at Sufferance: An estate arising when the tenant wrongfully holds over after the expiration of his term. The landlord has the choice of evicting the tenant as a trespasser or accepting such tenant for a similar term and under the conditions of the tenant's previous holding. Also called a Tenancy at Sufferance.

Estate of Will: The occupation of lands and tenements by a tenant for an indefinite period, terminable by one or both parties.

Estate for Years: An interest in lands by virtue of a contract for the possession of them for a definite and limited period of time. A lease may be said to be an estate for years.

Estimate: To form a preliminary opinion of value.

Estoppel: A doctrine which bars one from asserting rights which are inconsistent with a previous position or representation.

Eviction: Dispossession by process of law. The act of depriving a person of the possession of lands, in pursuance of the judgment of a court.

Exclusive Listing: A written agreement giving one agent the right to sell an owner's property and to collect a commission.

Exclusive Right to Sell Listing: A written instrument giving one agent the right to sell property for a specified time but reserving the right of the owner to sell the property without the payment of a commission.

George A. Cave

Execute: To complete, to make, to perform, to do, to follow out; to execute a deed, to make a deed, including especially signing, sealing, and delivery; to execute a contract is to perform the contract, to follow out to the end, to complete.

Executor: A person named in a will to carry out its provisions as to the disposition of the estate of a person deceased.

Expansible House: A home designed for further expansion and additions in the future.

Expansion Joint: A bituminous fiber strip used to separate units of concrete to prevent cracking due to expansion as a result of temperature changes.

Expenses: Certain items that may appear on a closing statement in connection with a real estate sale.

Extended Coverage: A broadened form of title insurance, or insurance in general.

Fair Market Value: This is the amount of money that would be paid for a property offered on the open market for a reasonable period of time with both buyer and seller knowing all the uses to which the property could be put and with neither party being under pressure to buy or sell.

Farmers Home Administration: An agency of the Department of Agriculture. Primary responsibility is to provide financial assistance for farmers and others living in rural areas where financing is not available on reasonable terms from private sources.

Federal Deposit Insurance Corporation: (FDIC) Agency of the federal government which insures deposits at commercial banks and savings banks.

Federal Home Loan Bank: (FHLB) A district bank of the Federal Home Loan Bank system that lends only to member savings and loan associations.

Federal Home Loan Bank Board: (FHLBB) The administrative agency that charters federal savings and loan associations and exercises regulatory authority over the FHLB system.

Federal Housing Administration: (FHA) An agency of the federal government that insures mortgage loans.

Federal National Mortgage Association: (FNMA) "Fanny Mae" a corporation (publicly traded on the New York Stock Exchange) whose primary function is to buy and sell FHA and VA mortgages in the secondary market.

Federal Saving and Loan Association: An association chartered by the FHLBB in contrast to a state-chartered savings and loan association.

Federal Savings and Loan Insurance Corporation: (FSLIC) An agency of the federal government that insures savers' accounts at savings and loan associations.

Fee Simple Absolute Estate: Ownership of title to real property. The greatest, most inclusive type of real estate ownership: without limitation or end: in perpetuity.

Fiduciary: Any person holding a position of trust such as an attorney, trustee, administrator, agent, or executor.

Financial Intermediary: Financial institutions such as commercial banks, savings and loan associations, mutual savings banks and life insurance companies which receive relatively small sums of money from the public and invest them in the form of large sums. A considerable portion of these funds are loaned on real estate.

Financing Statement: A form usually filed with the Secretary of State, giving the name and addresses of the debtor and the secured party, a description of the property used to secure the loan and sometimes the amount of the indebtedness. A public notice of a lien on personal property.

First Trust Deed: A legal document pledging collateral for a loan (see definition of Trust Deed), that has first priority over all other claims against the property except taxes and bonded indebtedness.

An Intelligent Approach to Buying Real Estate

Fiscal Controls: Federal tax revenue and expenditure policies used to control the level of economic activity.

Fixity of Location: The physical characteristics of real estate that subject it to the influence of its surroundings.

Fixture: Personal property permanently attached to land: improvement on real property considered part of real property.

Front Foot: A linear foot of property that runs along the street frontage which extends the depth of the property.

Foreclosure: Procedure whereby property pledged as security for a debt is sold to pay the debt in event of default in payments or terms.

Forfeiture: Loss of anything of value due to failure, on the part of one or more parties to a contract, to perform.

Foundation: The supporting portion of a structure below the first floor construction, or below grad, including the footings.

Franchise: A specified privilege awarded by a government or business firm which awards an exclusive dealership.

Fraud: The <u>intentional</u> and successful employment of any cunning, deception, collusion, or artifice, used to circumvent, cheat or deceive another person, whereby that person acts upon it to the loss of his property and to his legal injury.

George A. Cave

Freehold: An estate of indeterminable duration, such as fee simple or life estate.

Frontage: Land bordering a street.

Front Money: The minimum amount of money necessary to initiate a real estate venture.

Functional Obsolescence: A type of depreciation reflecting loss in value from out-of-date, old fashioned, or poorly designed equipment.

Gable Roof: A pitched roof with sloping sides.

Gambrel Roof: A curb roof, having a steep lower slope with a flatter upper slope above.

General Lien: A lien on all the property of a debtor. This type of lien is common in the event of losing a lawsuit in court. Instead of placing a lien on a specific property, a general lien is place on all properties a person may own. If any of the properties are sold or refinanced, the general lien will be paid off prior to the owner of the property receiving any funds.

G. I. Loans: A Federal Government guaranteed loan available to veterans under a program administered by the Veterans Administration.

Gift Deed: A deed for which the consideration is love and affection and where there isn't material consideration.

An Intelligent Approach to Buying Real Estate

Graduated Lease: Lease which provides for a varying rental rate, often based upon future determination; sometimes rent is based upon result of periodical appraisals; used largely in long-term leases.

Grant: A technical term made use of in deed of conveyance of lands to import a transfer.

Grant Deed: The customary document used in California to transfer title of real property. Contains two implied warranties that the owner has the right to sell and that there is no cloud on the title.

Grantee: The person to whom a grant is made, the purchaser.

Grantor: The person who makes the grant, the seller.

Gross income: Total income from property before any expenditures are deducted. An individual's income before deducting any taxes or other expenditures such as insurance and union dues.

Gross National Product: (GNP) the total value of all goods and services produced in an economy during a given period of time.

Gross Rate: A method of collecting interest by adding total interest to the principal of the loan at the outset of the term.

George A. Cave

Gross Rent Multiplier: A figure which, times the gross income of a property, produces an estimate of value of the property.

Ground Lease: An agreement for the use of the land only, sometimes secured by improvements placed on the land by the user.

Ground Rent: Earnings of improved property credited to earnings of the ground itself after allowance is made for earnings of improvements; often termed Economic Rent.

Guarantee of Title: A guarantee, backed only by the assets of reserves of the guarantor, given by a abstract company or title company that title is vested as shown on the guarantee. Guarantee of Title is not title insurance. (see Title Insurance)

Habendum Clause: The "to have and to hold" clause in a deed.

Header: A beam placed perpendicular to joists and to which joists are nailed in framing for chimney, stairway, or other opening.

Highest and Best Use: An appraisal phrase meaning that use which at the time of an appraisal is most likely to produce the greatest net return to the land and/or buildings over a given period of time; that use which will produce the greatest amount of amenities or profit. This is the starting point for appraisal.

An Intelligent Approach to Buying Real Estate

Hip Roof: A pitched roof with sloping sides and ends.

Holder in Due Course: One who has taken a note, check or bill of exchange in due course; 1) before it was overdue, 2) in good faith and for value, 3) without knowledge that it has been previously dishonored without notice of any defect at the time it was negotiated to him.

Holdover Tenant: Tenant who remains in possession of leased property after the expiration of the lease term.

Homestead: A limited exemption against certain money judgments, usually in a bankruptcy up to a certain amount, allowed a home owner. Also, a home upon which the owner has recorded a declaration of homestead.

Hundred Percent Location: A city retail business location which is considered the best available for attracting business.

Hypothecate: To designate certain property as security for a debt without giving up possession of it.

Impounds: A trust-type account established by lenders for the accumulation of funds to meet taxes, FHA mortgage insurance premiums, and /or future insurance policy premiums required to protect their security. Impounds are usually collected with the monthly mortgage payment.

George A. Cave

Improvement Cost: If a taxpayer makes a substantial improvement to a building, the improvement costs will be treated as a "separate building".

Income Approach: One of the three methods in the appraisal process; an analysis in which the estimated gross income from the subject residence is used as a basis for estimating value along with gross rent multipliers derived.

Indenture: A formal written instrument made between two or more persons in different interests.

Index: A measurement of interest rates used to determine the rate of interest charged in an adjustable rate loan.

Indirect Lighting: The light that is reflected from the ceiling or other object external to the fixture.

Injunction: A writ or order issued under the seal of a court to restrain one or more parties to a suit or proceeding from doing an act which is deemed to be inequitable or unjust in regard to the rights of some other party or parties in the suit or proceeding.

Installment Note: A note that provides that payments of a certain sum or amount be paid on the dates specified in the instrument.

An Intelligent Approach to Buying Real Estate

Installment Reporting: A method of reporting capital gains by installments for successive tax years to minimize the impact of the totality of the capital gains tax in the year of the sale.

Installment Sale: A sale wherein, for income tax purposes, the seller receives all or a portion of the proceeds of the sale in a year other than the year of sale.

Installment Sale Contract: See Conditional Sales Contract.

Institutional Lender: Any bank, insurance company, or savings and loan company which makes real estate loans.

Instrument: A written legal document; created to effect the rights of the parties.

Insurance: Protects the lien holders, the property owners and the occupants against loss due to fire, theft and a multitude of other possible losses. Mortgage holders require that a property be insured at least to the replacement value of the structures. Your personal residence would probably have the contents of the home insured as well.

Insurance also covers the homeowner in the event of an accident on his property. The insurance company pays not only the medical bills in the event a guest is injured but also the impending lawsuit.

In the case of rental properties, there is non-owner occupied insurance. That's where the structure is insured but the contents of the house are not. This policy also insures the landlord against lawsuit in the event a person is injured while on your property.

This type of insurance, for rental units, is less expensive than the homeowners policy one would have on their own home.

Interest: the charge in dollars for the use of money for a period of time. In a sense, the "rent" paid for the use of money.

Interest Rate: The rate that is charged to borrow money in terms of percentage.

Interim Loan: a short-term loan until long-term financing is available.

Intestate: a person who dies having made no will, or one which is defective in form in which case the estate descends to the heirs at law or next of kin.

Involuntary Lien: Any lien, such as a tax lien, judgment lien or mechanic's lien, legally imposed against property without the consent of the owner.

Irrigation Districts: Quasi-political districts created under special laws to provide for water services to property owners in the district; an operation governed to a great extent by law.

An Intelligent Approach to Buying Real Estate

Joint: The space between the adjacent surfaces of two components joined and held together by nails, glue, cement, or mortar.

Joint Note: A note signed by two or more persons who have equal liability for payment.

Joint and Severally Liable: A shared liability which provides that each party may be sued individually for the entire amount on a note, or that all parties may be sued jointly.

Joint Tenancy: A type of ownership of property by two or more people, all of which passes to the survivor(s) at the death of one of the others. This is a very common type of ownership for married couples, giving the property to the surviving spouse in the event of death. See also "Tenancy in Common".

Joint venture: Two or more individuals or firms joining together on a single project as partners.

Judgment: The final determination of a court in any legal matter presented to it for settlement.

Judgment Lien: A legal claim on all of the property of a judgment debtor which enables the judgment creditor to have the property sold for payment of the amount of the judgment.

Junior Mortgage: A mortgage second in lien to a previous mortgage.

George A. Cave

Jurisdiction: The authority by which judicial officers take cognizance of and decide causes; the power to hear and determine a cause; the right and power which a judicial officer has to enter upon the inquiry.

Laches: Delay or negligence in asserting one's legal rights.

Land and Improvement Loan: A loan obtained by the builder-developer for the purchase of land and to cover expenses for subdividing.

Land Contract: Same as Conditional Sales Contract.

Landlord: One who rents property to another.

Late Date Order: The commitment for an owner's title insurance policy issued by a title insurance company which covers the seller's title as of the date of the contract. When the sale closes the purchaser orders the title company to record the deed to purchaser and bring down their examination to cover this later date so as to show purchaser as owner of the property.

Lease: A contractual agreement between landlord and tenant whereby possession or use of land, or both, is transferred to the tenant for a limited period of time under certain specified conditions.

An Intelligent Approach to Buying Real Estate

Leasehold Estate: A tenant's right to occupy real estate during the term of the lease. This is a personal property interest.

Legal Description: A proper and formal method, recognized by law, of describing a particular parcel of real estate.

Lessor: (Landlord) The owner or trustee or real property who transfers the right to occupy and use real property to another by a lease.

Liabilities: Any claim held against a person or a corporation.

Lien: A claim against property which has been pledged or mortgaged to secure the performance of an obligation. Simply stated, in the event of the sale of a property, all liens on the property are paid off before the seller gets any money. Liens can be the mortgage, a tax bill that didn't get paid, a judgment from a lawsuit, etc. All can be placed on real property.

Life Estate: An estate or interest in real property which is held for the duration of the life of some certain person.

Limited Partnership: A partnership composed of some partners whose contribution and liability are limited.

Liquidated Damages: A specified sum of money to be paid under a contract in the event of a breach of the contract.

Lis Pendens: Suit pending, usually recorded so as to give constructive notice of pending litigation.

Listing: A written contract authorizing a broker to sell, buy or lease real property on behalf of another person, also known as an authorization to sell. Employment of an agent by a prospective purchaser or lessee to locate property for purchase or lease may be considered a listing.

Loan Administration: Mortgage bankers not only originate loans, but also "service" them from origination to maturity of the loan. Also called loan servicing.

Loan Application: A source of information on which the lender decides whether or not to make the loan, defines the terms of the loan contract; gives the name of the borrower, place or employment, salary history, bank accounts, and credit references; and describes the real estate that is to be mortgaged. It also stipulates the amount of loan being applied for and repayment terms.

Loan Commitment: Lender's contractual commitment to a loan based on the approval of the borrower's credit, the appraisal and the underwriting.

Loan Value: The value set, usually by a appraiser, to aid the lender in determining the amount of a new mortgage or trust deed loan.

An Intelligent Approach to Buying Real Estate

Loan Value-Ratio: The percentage of a property's value that a lender can or will loan to a borrower. For instance, if the ratio is 80 percent, then the lender will lend up to 80% of the appraised value of the property.

Margin of Security: The difference between the amount of the mortgage loan(s) and the appraised value of the property. May also be referred to as Equity.

Market Data Approach: A method of determining the appraised value of real property. (also see Comparative Analysis)

Market Price: The price paid regardless of pressures, motives, or intelligence.

Market Value: The price of which a specific property could be sold for on the open market provided there is a willing seller, a willing buyer, and the necessary amount of time to perform the sale.

Marketable Title: Property title, free of objectionable encumbrances and liens.

Material Fact: A fact is material if it is one which the agent should realize would be likely to affect the judgment of the principal in giving consent to the agent to enter into the particular transaction of the specified terms.

Mechanic's Lien: A statutory lien placed on a specific property to secure payment for labor or materials contributed to a work of improvement on that property.

Misplaced Improvements: Improvements of a property that do not conform to the most profitable use of the site.

Modular: A building composed of modules constructed on an assembly line in an off-sight factory. The modules are usually self-contained.

Monetary Controls: Federal Reserve tools for regulating the availability of money and credit to influence the level of economic activity.

Moratorium: A temporary suspension in the payment of a debt. There are times when a lender will allow a borrower to not make payments for a period of time. The Veterans Administration is famous for helping out veterans who have lost their jobs or have had an illness of the principal wage earner in the family. The VA are not the only ones who suspend payments for a time, conventional lenders will often do it as well. These lapses in payments are added to the end of the loan. If a problem should occur and you are incapable of making the payments contact your lender and ask them about suspension of the payments for a time. It never hurts to ask.

Mortgage: A conditional transfer of property to a creditor as security for the repayment of the debt. Simply stated, a loan on a property secured by a deed of trust.

An Intelligent Approach to Buying Real Estate

Mortgage Company: A state-regulated company that specializes in real estate loans that are readily salable in the secondary mortgage market.

Mortgage Guarantee Insurance: Insurance against financial loss available to mortgage lenders.

Mortgagee: A lender.

Mortgagor: A borrower.

Multiple Listing: A cooperative listing; usually an exclusive right to sell by a member of an organization of real estate brokers with the understanding that all members will have the opportunity to find an interested client.

Natural Person: A living person. Not a corporation.

Negotiable Instrument: A promissory note or check which meets certain legal requirements that allow it to circulate freely in commerce.

Net Listing: A listing which provides that the broker may retain as his commission that part of the sales price above a specified amount.

Net Worth: The differences between assets, including equity, and liabilities whether it be personal net worth or a business' net worth.

George A. Cave

Non-Institutional Lender: Sources of real estate loan funds other than lending institutions, such as union pension funds, endowed universities, and insurance companies.

Notary Public: An appointed officer with authority to take the acknowledgment of persons executing documents, to sign the certificate, and affix a notary seal.

Note: A signed written instrument acknowledging a debt and promising payment.

Notice of Abandonment: A document recorded to terminate a homestead

Notice of Completion: A notice placing time limits for mechanics' liens, which notice is recorded by the party who ordered the work or improvements.

Notice of Non-Responsibility: A notice which, when properly recorded and posted on the property, relieves the owner from the effect of mechanics' liens for work that was not ordered by the owner.

Notice To Pay Rent Or Quit: A 30-day notice required by law in most states before a tenant, delinquent in rental payments, may be evicted by court order (see Unlawful Detainer Action).

An Intelligent Approach to Buying Real Estate

Offset Statement: That statement of an owner or lender which sets forth the present status of any loan against the property. Also, a tenant's declaration of his interest in the property.

Open End Mortgage (or Trust Deed): A type of document which allows for future advances by using the same instrument for security. This type of a loan allows the borrower to borrow more money as the loan is paid down. Certain lines of credits use this type of mortgage as well.

Open Housing Law: Congress passed a law in April of 1968 that prohibits discrimination in the sale of real estate because of a buyer's race, color, or religion.

Option: A right given for a consideration to purchase or lease a property upon specified terms within a specific amount of time.

Oral Contract: A verbal agreement; one that has not been put in writing.

Orientation: The placing of a house on its lot with regard to its exposure to the rays of the sun, prevailing winds, privacy from the street and protection for outside noises.

"Or More": Important clause in a trust deed, or note, inclusion of which permits an early pay-off of the loan with or without penalty. (see Prepayment Penalty)

George A. Cave

Original Contractor: A contractor who contracts directly with the owner of real estate.

Over Improvement: An improvement which is not in the highest and best use of the site on which the improvement is placed by reason of excessive cost or size.

Partition Action: Court proceedings by which a co-owner is seeking to sever their joint ownership. For example, if two people own a property as "Tenants in Common", some event occurs such that owner "A" needs to have the house sold so he can get his share of any equity, but owner "B" does not want to sell. One option for owner "A" is to bring a partition action in order to force the sale.

Party Wall: A common wall constructed on the property line between two adjoining properties under different ownership, for the use of both properties.

Par Value: Market value, nominal value.

Patent: In real estate, the original conveyance or sale, of land from the federal government to a private owner.

Penalty: An extra payment or charge required of the borrower for deviating from the terms of the original loan agreement. Usually for being late in making the regular monthly payments or paying off a loan before it's due.

An Intelligent Approach to Buying Real Estate

Percentage Lease: A lease on a property, the rent for which is determined by the amount of business done by the lessee: usually a percentage of the gross receipts with a usual provision for a minimum amount of rent.

Perimeter Heating: Baseboard heating, or any system of heating in which the heat registers are located along the outside walls.

Personal Property: Any property that is not real property. Movable property is personal property. Fixtures within a structure that are attached to the structure are, in most instances, real property.

Pitch: The rise or incline of a roof.

Plaintiff: The party which initiates a lawsuit. The person claiming to be have been wronged

Planning Commission: A local government agency which plans proper physical growth of a community and recommends zoning ordinances and other laws for that purpose.

Points: A point is one percent of the amount of the loan, paid to the lender at the time the loan is made, in order to obtain the loan. In the Stock Market, a point means one dollar.

Police Power: The right reserved to the state to regulate the use of private property for the protection of the health, safety, morals, or general welfare of the public.

George A. Cave

Power of Attorney: Instrument used to appoint an attorney-in-fact, usually to act within certain specified limitations (limited power of attorney) on certain specified matters.

Power of sale Clause: A clause in a trust deed which gives the trustee the right to sell borrower's property publicly, without court procedure, if the borrower defaults, or if included in a mortgage, to permit the lender to foreclose without court procedure.

Prepaid Items of Expense: Prorations of prepaid items of expense that are credited to the seller in the closing statement. For example, in the case of impound for taxes and insurance. The seller has a requirement to keep several months of payments in an impound account. These prepaid impounds are generally paid to the seller at the close of escrow. This is a general practice and not a law. When purchasing property, state on the purchase contract that the impounds will be given "gratis" to the seller.

Prepayment Penalty: A clause in a note which provides for a penalty in the event of an early pay-off of the note. Prepayment penalties have been severely limited by legislation in recent years.

Primary Financing: That trust deed and note which has first priority. Priority is assigned by the order in which deeds and liens are filed. They are paid in the same order.

An Intelligent Approach to Buying Real Estate

Primary Mortgage Market: The market where loans are made directly to borrowers.

Principal: 1) Capital or money which is loaned as a debt where interest is charged. 2) An individual mainly liable for a contract or other obligation. One who engages another to act as their representative. (A person wishing to sell their home may employ the services of an agent or Realtor. In this case the person selling the home is the principal.)

Promissory Note: A written contract containing a promise to pay a specified amount of money at a specified future time.

Property: The rights of ownership. The right to use, possess, enjoy and dispose of a thing in every legal way and to exclude everyone else from interfering with these rights. Property is generally classified into two groups, personal property and real property.

Prorations: Adjustment of interest, taxes, and insurance, on a prorata basis as of the closing date.

Purchase Contract and Receipt For Deposit: The formal name of the contract used to accept "earnest money" that will bind an offer for purchase of property by a prospective buyer.

Purchase Money: An obligation of money on paper as in a deed of trust, mortgage or land contract given to the seller to secure payment of the balance of the purchase price, or a deed of trust, mortgage or land contract on an owner-occupied dwelling of four units or less, given to a lender to secure repayment of a loan that was used to purchase the property. Not actual cash as in a down payment.

Quiet Title Action: A suit brought for the purpose of establishing clear title to real property or to remove a cloud on the title.

Quitclaim Deed: A deed containing no warranties of any kind used to transfer any interest in real property which the grantor may have.

Range: A strip of land six miles wide determined by a government survey, running in a north to south direction.

Real Property: Land, including all that is affixed to it. This includes anything that is attached to the dwelling including light fixtures, floor covering, cabinets, doors, built-in appliances, heating and air conditioners, etc.

Note: In the event that a person wishes to sell a piece of real property and wishes to retain certain pieces or fixtures of that property, it should be so stipulated in the purchase contract.

For instance, if while selling your home, there is some reason you wish to retain some of the light fixtures. (Maybe they have been in your family for years and hold some sentimental value to you.) Those lights, if affixed to the structure, are part of that structure and must be stipulated in the purchase contract. If the contract doesn't say otherwise,

An Intelligent Approach to Buying Real Estate

everything attached to the dwelling is being sold as a part of the real property.

Realtor: Any member of any local Real Estate Board affiliated with the National Association of Realtors.

Reconveyance: The transfer of the title of land from one person to the immediate preceding owner. This particular instrument of transfer is commonly used when the performance or debt is settled under the terms of a deed of trust, when the trustee conveys the title that was being held on condition back to the owner.

Record: To file for record in the office of the County Recorder. Giving public constructive notice of the contents of the document. Most real estate documents are recorded. However, a deed does not need to be recorded to be valid.

Redemption: Buying back one's property after a judicial sale, such as a foreclosure.

Refinancing: The paying off of an exiting mortgage(s) and assuming a new mortgage in it's place.

Rehabilitation: The restoration of a property to a satisfactory condition, usable for its intended purpose, without drastically changing the floor plan, form or style of architecture.

Regression: An appraising principle that holds that if a high-valued property is placed, or constructed, in a neighborhood of lower-valued property it seeks the level of the lower-valued property.

Release Clause: A stipulation in a trust deed or mortgage which provides that a specific described lot or area will be removed from the blanket lien upon the payment of a specific sum of money.

Replacement Cost: A method of appraising a property on the basis of producing an exact replica.

Reproduction Cost: The cost of reproducing a new replica property on the basis of current prices with the same or closely similar materials.

Request For Notice of Default: A recorded notice made by the beneficiary of a trust deed, which requests that he be notified in the event that foreclosure proceedings are commenced by any other party of interest.

Rescind: To cancel a contract from the beginning, thus restoring the parties to their original positions.

Restriction: An encumbrance which limits the use of real estate in some way.

Rider: Any addition, amendment, or endorsement to a document. Something added later.

An Intelligent Approach to Buying Real Estate

Right-of-way: An easement giving a person the right to pass over the land of another.

Riparian Rights: The right of a landowner to that water on, under, or adjacent to his land.

Satisfaction: The discharge of a mortgage or trust deed lien from the records upon payment of the evidenced debt.

Secondary Mortgage: A loan secured by a second mortgage or trust deed on real property. These could be second, third, fourth, fifth, etc.

Secondary Mortgage Market: Market place for the sale and purchase of existing trust deeds and mortgages. Not to be mistaken for second mortgages. This market is in the business of buying and selling existing loans. For instance, real estate may be moving slowing in Texas but is moving very quickly in California. The loans originate in California and are purchased by lending institutions in Texas.

Section: One square mile of land, 640 acres.

Security Agreement: An agreement which creates or provides for a security interest. The form used to give a lender an interest in whatever personal property is being used to secure the loan.

Separate Property: Property owned by a husband and wife which is not Community Property. In a community property state like California, all moneys made from income after marriage is community property. Real property that is purchased with community property is then also community property.

Real estate purchased without money could be construed as personal property as long as the upkeep on that property is not paid for with community funds. If a property is purchased as "Sole and Separate Property" in most community property states, the title company will require the non-titled spouse to sign a "Disclaimer" stating that he/she has no interest in the property.

The first dozen properties I purchased, my wife, now ex-wife, wanted nothing to do with them and signed disclaimers on them all. When we went to get divorced, she decided that she was now interested in the properties. The court decided that since the properties were purchased with my ingenuity, in other words "no money down", then the properties were indeed separate property.

Septic Tank: An underground tank in which sewage from the house is reduced to liquid by bacterial action and drained off. (If at all possible, purchase property that is connected to the city sewer system. Septic tanks are just one more headache to worry about.)

Servicing: The administering of a loan after it has been made. Includes the collection of the payments, keeping accounting records, computing the interest and principal, foreclosure of defaulted loans, and so on.

An Intelligent Approach to Buying Real Estate

Setback Ordinance: Any law prohibiting the erection of a building or any structure within a certain distance from the curb.

Severalty Ownership: Owned by only one person; sole ownership.

Sheriff's Deed: Deed given by court order in connection with sale of property to satisfy a judgment.

Short Rate: The disproportionate amount of an insurance premium that is returned when an insured cancels his policy. The insurance company retains a portion of the unused premium as a cancellation penalty.

Sinking Fund: A fund set aside from the income of a property which, with accrued interest, will pay for the repairs and maintenance of the structure.

Special Assessment: A special tax against real estate levied by a public authority to pay the cost of such public improvements of the property such as sewers, curb and gutter, street lights, etc.

Special Warranty Deed: A deed in which the grantor warrants or guarantees the title only against defects arising during his or her ownership of the property and not against defects existing before the time of his or her ownership.

Spread: In an Adjustable Rate Mortgage a spread is the difference between the index and the amount of interest charged. For instance, the "index" for an ARM may be the prime lending rate and the "spread" is 3%. If the prime rate is 4%, then the interest rate charged on the loan would be 7% (4% plus 3%). As the prime rate changes the interest rate on the loan will change at some restated interval so that it is always 3% above the prime rate.

There are maximum amounts of increase in an ARM, the cap, and also a maximum amount of decrease in the interest rate of an ARM. (see Adjustable Rate Mortgage, Index, Cap)

Standard Form: A basic-policy form of title insurance which is usually issued to the purchaser of real estate.

State Housing Law: That state law, in most states, which sets minimum building standards throughout the state.

Statute of Frauds: State law which provides that certain contracts must be in writing in order to be enforceable by law. Examples would be a real property lease for longer than one year or an agent's authorization to sell real estate.

Statutory Warranty Deed: A short form warranty deed which warrants by inference that the seller is the undisputed owner and has the right to convey the property and that the owner will defend the title if necessary. This type of deed protects the buyer in that the seller agrees to defend all claims against the property. If the seller fails to do so, the new owner can defend his claims and sue the former owner.

An Intelligent Approach to Buying Real Estate

Subdivision: Division of land into a certain number of parcels with the intent to sell, lease or finance, now or at any time in the future.

Sublease: A lease given by someone who himself is leasing the property. This is one way that some people enjoy the benefits of being a landlord without owning property. Many landlords are so by not fault of their own. They may have wanted to by a bigger house and have been unable to sell their previous home, or maybe they are just waiting for a better market to sell it in. Sometimes people just make bad landlords and will lease their home to someone at a very low price and then the lease holder can turn around and rent it out to someone else at a higher price. This is called subleasing. The owner is still responsible for the maintenance on the property but the original lease holder is responsible for his new renters and any damage that they might do. Also if the sublessee does not pay the rent, the original lease holder still has to pay it.

Subordination Clause: A clause benefiting the borrower in a mortgage or trust deed by which the lender relinquishes his priority to a subsequent mortgage or trust deed. This is not uncommon in owner financing, where the previous owner carried a note back and the current owner wishes to refinance the existing loan. The previous owner could agree to let the new loan take a position in front of his by way of a subordination clause.

George A. Cave

Take-Out Loan: A long-term loan that replaces an interim construction loan.

Tax Deed: That deed given when property is sold to satisfy a tax delinquency.

Tax Free Exchange: A method of deferring income taxes on capital gains by exchanging real property for other like property. Referred to as a "Tax Shelter"

Tax Sale: Sale of property after a period of nonpayment of taxes.

Tenancy in Common: Ownership by two or more persons who hold undivided interest, <u>without</u> the right of survivorship. Interests in the property need not be equal.

Time Is Of The Essence: One of the essential requirements to the forming of a binding contract which contemplates a punctual performance.

Title: An instrument showing evidence of ownership of land is entitled to legal possession of that land.

Title Insurance: Insurance to protect property owner(s) against loss if title is imperfect.

Title Report: A report that discloses condition of the title, made by a title company preliminary to issuance of title insurance.

An Intelligent Approach to Buying Real Estate

Tort: A wrongful act; wrongful injury; violation of a legal right.

Township: A 36-square-mile unit of land six miles long on each side.

Trade Fixtures: Articles of personal property annexed (affixed) to real property, but which are necessary to the carrying on of a trade and are removable by the owner.

Trade-In: A method of guaranteeing an owner a minimum amount of cash upon the sale of his present property to permit the purchase of another. If the property is not sold within a specified time at the listed price, the broker agrees to arrange financing to purchase the property at a previously agreed-upon price

Trust Account: An account separate, apart and physically segregated form the broker's personal funds, in which the broker is required, by law, to deposit all funds collected for his clients.

Trust Deed (Deed of Trust): A deed by which a Trustor conveys his title to the trustee as security for the payment of a debt.

Trustee: One who holds legal title to property for a special purpose without being the actual (beneficial) owner. A trustee is one of the parties to every trust deed.

George A. Cave

Trustee's Deed: Deed given by the trustee when property is sold under the power of sale in a trust deed.

Trustor: Borrower in a trust deed. One who deeds his property to the trustee in a trust deed transaction.

Underwriting: The technical analysis by a lender to determine the borrower's ability to repay a contemplated loan.

Undue Influence: Taking any fraudulent or unfair advantage of an other's weakness of mind, or distress or necessity.

Unearned Increment: An increase in the value of property, not anticipated by the owner and resulting primarily from the operation of social forces. Often due to increase in population or desirability of a specific area or location.

Uniform Commercial Code: A form of statutory law that covers a number of areas of commercial law, including laws concerning sales contracts and warranties. The UCC has been adopted in its entirety in forty-nine states, and about half in Louisiana.

Unlawful Detained Action: Lawsuit brought to evict a tenant who unlawfully remains in possession of real property.

Unruh Act: In California, that law which prohibits discrimination by agents or business establishments because of race, color, creed, or national origin.

An Intelligent Approach to Buying Real Estate

Usury: Stating the maximum amount of interest that can be claimed by a person, not a lending institution, currently at 12 percent. This is the only limitation on owner financing. The maximum percentage rate allowed to be charged by an owner on an owner-carried note is 12%. This rate is subject to change by law.

Utility: Usability. One of the four essential elements of value

Value: The worth of a thing in money or goods at a certain time.

Variance: Change in zoning of a single parcel. Called "legal non-conforming" in some states.

Warranty Deed: A deed used to convey real property which contains warranties of title and quiet possession, and the grantor thus agrees to defend the premises against the lawful claim of third persons. It is commonly used in many states, but in others the grant deed has supplanted it due to the modern practice of securing title insurance policies which have reduced the importance of expressed and implied warranty in deeds.

Wraparound Mortgage: It involves the borrower entering into a second, or subsequent mortgage. This arrangement represents the means by which the borrower can add to development without refinancing the first mortgage at substantially higher current interest rates. For instance, you sell a property to a buyer and are going to carry $10,000 as an owner financed loan. The first mortgage is $70,000 at an interest rate of 7%. This along with the $10,000 that you are going to carry, creates a balance of $80,000. You "wrap" the entire amount, $80,000, at an interest rate of 8 1/2% (or any rate that you and the buyer should decide upon). You would then make 8 1/2% on the $10,000 that the buyer owes to you and you would also make 1 1/2% on the original $70,000. One monthly payment should be made, by the buyer, to a title company, who would in turn send a check to the original lender for the amount of its monthly payment and send a check to you for the balance.

AMORTIZATION SCHEDULE PER $1000
AMORTIZATION IN YEARS

APR	1	2	3	4	5	6
5%	85.61	43.88	29.98	23.03	18.18	16.11
5 1/4%	85.73	43.99	30.09	23.15	18.99	16.23
5 1/2%	85.84	44.10	30.20	23.26	19.11	16.34
5 3/4%	85.96	44.21	30.31	23.38	19.22	16.46
6%	86.06	44.33	30.43	23.49	19.34	16.58
6 1/4%	86.19	44.44	30.54	23.60	19.45	16.70
6 1/2%	86.30	44.55	30.65	23.72	19.57	16.81
6 3/4%	86.42	44.66	30.77	23.84	19.69	16.93
7%	86.85	44.78	30.88	23.95	19.81	17.05
7 1/8%	86.59	44.83	30.94	24.01	19.87	17.11
7 1/4%	86.65	44.89	31.00	24.07	19.92	17.17
7 3/8%	86.70	44.95	31.05	24.13	19.98	17.23
7 1/2%	86.76	45.00	31.11	24.18	20.04	17.30
7 5/8%	86.82	45.06	31.17	24.24	20.10	17.36
7 3/4%	86.88	45.12	331.23	24.30	20.16	17.42
7 7/8%	86.94	45.18	31.28	24.36	20.22	17.48
8%	86.99	45.23	31.34	24.42	20.28	17.54
8 1/8%	87.05	45.29	31.40	24.48	20.34	17.60
8 1/4%	87.11	45.35	31.46	24.54	20.40	17.66
8 3/8%	87.17	45.40	31.51	24.59	20.46	17.72
8 1/2%	87.22	45.46	31.57	24.65	20.52	17.78
8 5/8%	87.28	45.52	31.63	24.71	20.58	17.84
8 3/4%	87.34	45.58	31.69	24.77	20.64	17.91
8 7/8%	87.40	45.63	31.75	24.83	20.70	17.97
9	87.46	45.69	31.80	24.89	20.76	18.03
9 1/8%	87.51	45.75	31.86	24.95	20.82	18.09
9 1/4%	87.57	45.80	31.92	25.01	20.88	18.15
9 3/8%	87.63	45.86	31.98	25.07	20.95	18.22
9 1/2%	87.69	45.92	32.04	25.13	21.01	18.28
9 5/8%	87.75	45.98	32.10	25.19	21.07	18.34
9 3/4%	87.80	46.03	32.15	25.25	21.13	18.41
9 7/8%						
10	87.92	46.15	32.27	25.37	21.25	18.53
10 1/4%	88.04	46.27	32.39	25.49	21.38	18.66
10 1/2%	88.15	46.38	32.51	25.61	21.50	18.78
10 3/4%	88.27	46.50	32.63	25.73	21.62	18.91
11	88.39	46.61	32.74	25.85	21.75	19.04
11 1/4%	88.50	46.73	32.86	25.97	21.87	19.17
11 1/2%	88.62	46.85	32.98	26.09	22.00	19.30
11 3/4%	88.74	46.96	33.10	26.22	22.12	19.43
12%	88.85	47.08	33.22	26.34	22.25	19.56

AMORTIZATION SCHEDULE PER $1000
AMORTIZATION IN YEARS

APR	7	8	9	10	11	12
5%	14.14	12.66	11.52	10.61	9.87	9.25
5 1/4%	14.26	12.78	11.64	10.73	9.99	9.38
5 1/2%	14.38	12.90	11.76	10.86	10.12	9.51
5 3/4%	14.49	13.03	11.89	10.98	10.25	9.63
6%	14.61	13.15	12.01	11.11	10.37	9.76
6 1/4%	14.73	13.27	12.13	11.23	10.50	9.89
6 1/2%	14.85	13.39	12.26	11.36	10.63	10.02
6 3/4%	14.98	13.51	12.39	11.49	10.76	10.16
7%	15.10	13.64	12.51	11.62	10.89	10.29
7 1/8%	15.16	13.70	12.57	11.68	10.95	10.36
7 1/4%	15.22	13.76	12.64	11.75	10.42	9.92
7 3/8%	15.28	13.83	12.70	11.81	11.09	10.49
7 1/2%	15.34	13.89	12.77	11.88	11.15	10.56
7 5/8%	15.41	13.95	12.83	11.94	11.22	10.62
7 3/4%	15.47	14.01	12.89	12.01	11.29	10.69
7 7/8%	15.53	14.08	12.96	12.07	11.35	10.76
8%	15.59	14.14	13.02	12.14	11.42	10.83
8 1/8%	15.65	14.21	13.09	12.20	11.49	10.90
8 1/4%	15.72	14.27	13.15	12.27	11.56	10.97
8 3/8%	15.78	14.33	13.22	12.34	11.62	11.04
8 1/2%	15.84	14.40	13.28	12.40	11.69	11.11
8 5/8%	15.90	14.46	13.35	12.47	11.76	11.18
8 3/4%	15.97	14.53	13.42	12.54	11.83	11.24
8 7/8%	16.03	14.59	13.48	12.61	11.90	11.32
9	16.09	14.66	13.55	12.67	11.97	11.39
9 1/8%	16.16	14.72	13.61	12.74	12.03	11.46
9 1/4%	16.22	14.79	13.68	12.81	12.10	11.53
9 3/8%	16.29	14.85	13.75	12.88	12.17	11.60
9 1/2%	16.35	14.92	13.81	12.94	12.24	11.67
9 5/8%	16.41	14.98	13.88	13.01	12.31	11.74
9 3/4%	16.48	15.05	13.95	13.08	12.38	11.81
9 7/8%	16.54	15.11	14.02	13.15	12.45	11.88
10	16.61	15.18	14.08	13.22	12.52	11.96
10 1/4%	16.74	15.31	14.22	13.36	12.67	12.10
10 1/2%	16.87	15.45	14.36	13.50	12.81	12.25
10 3/4%	17.00	15.58	14.49	13.64	12.95	12.39
11	17.13	15.71	14.63	13.78	13.10	12.54
11 1/4%	17.26	15.85	14.77	13.92	13.24	12.69
11 1/2%	17.39	15.98	14.91	14.06	13.39	12.84
11 3/4%	17.52	16.12	15.05	14.21	13.54	12.99
12%	17.66	16.26	15.19	14.35	13.68	13.14

AMORTIZATION SCHEDULE PER $1000
AMORTIZATION IN YEARS

APR	13	14	15	16	17	18
5%	8.74	8.29	7.91	7.58	7.29	7.04
5 1/4%	8.86	8.42	8.04	7.71	7.43	7.17
5 1/2%	8.99	8.55	8.18	7.85	7.56	7.31
5 3/4%	9.12	8.68	8.31	7.98	7.70	7.45
6%	9.25	8.82	8.44	8.12	7.84	7.59
6 1/4%	9.38	8.95	8.58	8.26	7.98	7.73
6 1/2%	9.52	9.09	8.72	8.40	8.12	7.87
6 3/4%	9.65	9.22	8.85	8.54	8.26	8.01
7%	9.79	9.36	8.99	8.68	8.40	8.16
7 1/8%	9.85	9.43	9.06	8.75	8.47	8.23
7 1/4%	9.92	9.50	9.13	8.82	8.55	8.31
7 3/8%	9.99	9.57	9.20	8.89	8.62	8.38
7 1/2%	10.06	9.64	9.28	8.96	8.69	8.45
7 5/8%	10.13	9.71	9.35	9.04	8.77	8.53
7 3/4%	10.20	9.78	9.42	9.11	8.84	8.60
7 7/8%	10.27	9.85	9.49	9.18	8.91	8.68
8%	10.34	9.92	9.56	9.25	8.99	8.75
8 1/8%	10.41	9.99	9.63	9.33	9.06	8.83
8 1/4%	10.48	10.06	9.71	9.40	9.14	8.91
8 3/8%	10.55	10.13	9.78	9.48	9.21	8.98
8 1/2%	10.62	10.20	9.85	9.55	9.29	9.06
8 5/8%	10.69	10.28	9.93	9.62	9.36	9.14
8 3/4%	10.76	10.35	10.00	9.70	9.44	9.21
8 7/8%	10.83	10.42	10.07	9.77	9.52	9.29
9	10.90	10.49	10.15	9.85	9.59	9.37
9 1/8%	10.97	10.57	10.22	9.93	9.67	9.45
9 1/4%	11.05	10.64	10.30	10.00	9.75	9.53
9 3/8%	11.12	10.71	10.37	10.08	9.82	9.61
9 1/2%	11.19	10.79	10.45	10.15	9.90	9.68
9 5/8%	11.26	10.86	10.52	10.23	9.98	9.76
9 3/4%	11.34	10.94	10.60	10.31	10.06	9.84
9 7/8%	11.41	11.01	10.67	10.39	10.14	9.92
10	11.48	11.09	10.75	10.46	10.22	10.00
10 1/4%	11.63	11.24	10.90	10.62	10.38	10.16
10 1/2%	11.78	11.39	11.06	10.78	10.54	10.33
10 3/4%	11.93	11.54	11.21	10.94	10.70	10.49
11	12.08	11.70	11.37	11.10	10.86	10.66
11 1/4%	12.23	11.85	11.53	11.26	11.02	10.82
11 1/2%	12.38	12.01	11.69	11.42	11.19	10.99
11 3/4%	12.54	12.16	11.85	11.58	11.35	11.16
12%	12.69	12.32	12.01	11.74	11.52	11.32

AMORTIZATION SCHEDULE PER $1000
AMORTIZATION IN YEARS

APR	19	20	21	22	23	24
5%	6.81	6.60	6.42	6.26	6.11	5.97
5 1/4%	6.95	6.74	6.56	6.40	6.25	6.12
5 1/2%	7.08	6.88	6.70	6.54	6.40	6.27
5 3/4%	7.22	7.03	6.85	6.69	6.54	6.41
6%	7.37	7.17	6.99	6.84	6.69	6.56
6 1/4%	7.51	7.31	7.14	6.98	6.84	6.72
6 1/2%	7.65	7.46	7.29	7.13	7.00	6.87
6 3/4%	7.80	7.61	7.44	7.29	7.15	7.03
7%	7.95	7.76	7.59	7.44	7.30	7.18
7 1/8%	8.02	7.83	7.67	7.52	7.38	7.26
7 1/4%	8.10	7.91	7.74	7.59	7.46	7.34
7 3/8%	8.17	7.98	7.82	7.67	7.54	7.42
7 1/2%	8.25	8.06	7.90	7.75	7.62	7.50
7 5/8%	8.32	8.14	7.97	7.83	7.70	7.58
7 3/4%	8.40	8.21	8.05	7.91	7.78	7.66
7 7/8%	8.47	8.29	8.13	7.99	7.86	7.74
8%	8.55	8.37	8.21	8.07	7.94	7.83
8 1/8%	8.63	8.45	8.29	8.15	8.02	7.91
8 1/4%	8.70	8.53	8.37	8.23	8.10	7.99
8 3/8%	8.78	8.60	8.45	8.31	8.18	8.07
8 1/2%	8.86	8.68	8.53	8.39	8.27	8.16
8 5/8%	8.94	8.76	8.61	8.47	8.35	8.24
8 3/4%	9.02	8.84	8.69	8.55	8.43	8.32
8 7/8%	9.09	8.92	8.77	8.63	8.51	8.41
9	9.17	9.00	8.85	8.72	8.60	8.49
9 1/8%	9.25	9.08	8.93	8.80	8.68	8.58
9 1/4%	9.33	9.16	9.01	8.88	8.77	8.66
9 3/8%	9.41	9.24	9.10	8.97	8.85	8.75
9 1/2%	9.49	9.33	9.18	9.05	8.93	8.83
9 5/8%	9.57	9.41	9.26	9.13	9.02	8.92
9 3/4%	9.65	9.49	9.35	9.22	9.11	9.01
9 7/8%	9.74	9.57	9.43	9.30	9.19	9.09
10	9.82	9.66	9.51	9.39	9.28	9.18
10 1/4%	9.98	9.82	9.68	9.56	9.45	9.35
10 1/2%	10.15	9.99	9.85	9.73	9.62	9.53
10 3/4%	10.31	10.16	10.02	9.90	9.80	9.71
11	10.48	10.33	10.19	10.08	9.98	9.89
11 1/4%	10.65	10.50	10.37	10.25	10.15	10.06
11 1/2%	10.82	10.67	10.54	10.43	10.33	10.25
11 3/4%	10.99	10.84	10.72	10.61	10.51	10.43
12%	11.16	11.02	10.89	10.78	10.69	10.6

AMORTIZATION SCHEDULE PER $1000
AMORTIZATION IN YEARS

APR	25	26	29	30	35	40
5%	5.85	5.74	5.45	5.37	5.05	4.83
5 1/4%	6.00	5.89	5.61	5.53	5.21	4.99
5 1/2%	6.15	6.04	5.76	5.68	5.38	5.16
5 3/4%	6.30	6.19	5.92	5.84	5.54	5.33
6%	6.45	6.34	6.08	6.00	5.71	5.51
6 1/4%	6.60	6.50	6.24	6.16	5.88	5.68
6 1/2%	6.76	6.65	6.40	6.33	6.05	5.86
6 3/4%	6.91	6.81	6.56	6.49	6.22	6.04
7%	7.07	6.97	6.73	6.67	6.39	6.22
7 1/8%	7.15	7.05	6.81	6.74	6.48	6.31
7 1/4%	7.23	7.14	6.89	6.83	6.57	6.40
7 3/8%	7.31	7.22	6.98	6.91	6.67	6.49
7 1/2%	7.39	7.30	7.06	7.00	6.75	6.59
7 5/8%	7.48	7.38	7.15	7.08	6.84	6.68
7 3/4%	7.56	7.46	7.23	7.17	6.93	6.77
7 7/8%	7.64	7.55	7.32	7.26	7.02	6.86
8%	7.72	7.63	7.40	7.34	7.11	6.96
8 1/8%	7.81	7.71	7.49	7.43	7.20	7.05
8 1/4%	7.89	7.80	7.58	7.52	7.29	7.15
8 3/8%	7.97	7.88	7.67	7.61	7.38	7.24
8 1/2%	8.06	7.97	7.75	7.69	7.47	7.34
8 5/8%	8.14	8.05	7.84	7.78	7.57	7.43
8 3/4%	8.23	8.14	7.93	7.87	7.66	7.53
8 7/8%	8.31	8.23	8.02	7.96	7.75	7.62
9	8.40	8.31	8.11	8.05	7.84	7.72
9 1/8%	8.48	8.40	8.20	8.14	7.94	7.81
9 1/4%	8.57	8.49	8.29	8.23	8.03	7.91
9 3/8%	8.66	8.57	8.38	8.32	8.13	8.01
9 1/2%	8.74	8.66	8.47	8.41	8.22	8.11
9 5/8%	8.83	8.75	8.56	8.50	8.32	8.20
9 3/4%	8.92	8.84	8.65	8.60	8.41	8.30
9 7/8%	9.00	8.93	8.74	8.69	8.51	8.40
10	9.09	9.01	8.83	8.78	8.60	8.50
10 1/4%	9.27	9.19	9.01	8.97	8.79	8.69
10 1/2%	9.45	9.37	9.20	9.15	8.99	8.89
10 3/4%	9.63	9.55	9.38	9.34	9.18	9.09
11	9.81	9.74	9.57	9.53	9.37	9.29
11 1/4%	9.99	9.92	9.76	9.72	9.57	9.49
11 1/2%	10.17	10.10	9.95	9.91	9.77	9.69
11 3/4%	10.35	10.29	10.14	10.10	9.96	9.89
12%	10.54	10.47	10.33	10.29	10.16	10.09

INDEX

Accelerated depreciation, 100
Adjusted rate mortgage, ARM, 32
Air conditioning, 97, 99
Air Force, 11, 60
Allowance, 82
    decorating, 82
    landscaping, 82
Alternate financing, 21, 22
Appliance(s), 97, 99
Appreciation, 5, 63
Appraisal, 38, 41
Arbitrator, 104, 105, 106, 107, 108
Arizona, 96
Authorized lender, 41, 65
Auto pay plan, 23
Balloon payment, 51, 52, 53, 54, 57
Bankruptcy, 6, 34, 65
Beast Next Door, The, 77
Break even cash flow, 11
Broker, 37, 61, 62
Buyers agent, 37
By owner, 77
Caesar, 108
California, 9, 11, 19, 22, 36, 70, 77
California Assoc. of Realtors, 19
Cap, 33
Carpet, 25, 26, 36, 97, 99

Cash flow, 53
CTM(cash to mortgage, 70
Certificate of eligibility, 40
Closing costs, 19, 35, 50, 63, 78
Collection agency, 22
Commission, 36, 37, 50, 61, 63
Compound interest,
Condominiums, 23, 27, 67, 70
Continental Lawyer's Title, 31
Conventional foreclosures, 65
Conventional loan, 21, 42, 43, 44
Creative Financing, 45
Credit report, 21, 52
Credit reporting agency, 52
DD Form 214, 40
Deed in lieu of foreclosure, 52, 54
Default, 34, 74
Deductible, 94, 95, 96, 98, 100, 105
Depreciation, 94 -100
Distressed properties, 17
Distressed seller(s), 47, 66
Distressed property(ies), 17
District fund rate, 32, 33
Double close, 83
Due on sale clause, 74
Duplex, 7, 49, 52
Economic Indicator, 32

Entertainment expense, 97
Entitlement, 42
Escrow instructions, 20
Escrow officer, 20, 76
Estate planning, 7
Eviction notice,
FHA, 21, 31, 32, 33, 34, 35, 36, 39, 41, 43, 47, 64, 65
FHA financing, 33
FHA foreclosures, 64
FHA loan, 34, 35, 37, 38, 40, 44, 51
FHA Title I loan, 38
Financial advisor, 16
Financing, 30, 43, 68, 73
Fix-up, 17, 38, 52
Fixed rate loan, 32
Foreclosure(s), 52, 54, 56, 57, 66, 67, 86
Funding fee, 39
GI Bill, 9, 40, 60
Government guaranteed loan, 21
Graduated payments, 32, 53
Graffiti, 29
Handyman, 28
Home Depot, 99
Homeowners association, 27, 71
Homeowners fees, 23, 71, 94
Hotel liquidators, 25, 26
Income taxes, 13, 95
Income to mortgage ratio, 34, 65
Index, 32, 33
Inspection, 35
Institutional lender, 66, 67
Insurance, 7, 12, 20, 23, 34, 61, 69, 94, 98
Interest, 20, 23, 107
Internal Revenue Service(IRS), 28, 69, 95, 97, 98, 99, 101, 102, 103, 104, 105, 106, 108
Internet, 40
Jimmy Carter, 32
Landlord, 27, 89, 91, 92, 93, 108

Lease, 86
Ledger, 103, 104
Lender's report, 31, 35, 41, 44
Lender's survey, 31
Leverage, 6, 31
Listing agent, 37
Listing broker, 37
Loan guarantee, 41
Los Angeles, 10
Los Angeles Times, 33
Maintenance factor, 23, 24
Management, 94
Management company, 28
Modeling, 46
Mortgage insurance(MIP), 34, 35
Mortgage ratio, 19
Motivated seller, 51, 66
Mutual fund, 14, 16, 30, 31, 50
Negative amortization, 54
Negative cash flow, 11, 12
Negotiate, 18, 35, 37, 55, 72, 75, 78
Net operating income, 89
Newbury Park, 9
Nike, 16
No money down, 7, 9, 10, 17, 39, 40, 42, 47, 51, 64, 77, 78
Oregon, 77, 79
Origination fee, 63
Owner carry back, 45, 47, 49, 52, 53, 76
Owner financing, 45, 76
Passive investor, 28
Personal referrals, 25
Pest control, 99
Peter Lynch, 14, 16
Phoenix, 11, 22, 25, 26, 47, 58, 59, 61, 70, 85, 98
P&I, 20
PITI, 23, 50, 61, 74
Point(s), 33, 43
Polaroid, 59
Positive cash flow, 12, 22, 23, 28, 50, 55, 63, 71, 72, 90

Pre-approved, 35, 40
Prime rate, 33
Preliminary Title report, 69
Principal, 20, 23, 43, 52, 61, 76
Property taxes, 94
Prorate(d), 62
Purchase contract, 19, 20, 37, 47, 74, 82
Qualify, 34
Quicken, 73
Re-negotiate, 52
Realtor, 8, 9, 10, 19, 20, 36, 41, 47, 49, 51, 78, 93
Reconveyance, 76
REO, 65, 66
Replacement, 25, 99
Referral, 92
Refinance, 43, 83
Refrigerator, 26
Retirement income, 13,
Retirement account, 13
Roof, 25, 26, 48, 60, 97, 99
Savings plan, 14
Schedule C, 100
Schedule E, 100
Sears, 26
Section 8, government lease, 26, 29, 61, 87
Selling broker, 37
Spread, 33
Stipulation, 107
Stock market, 16
Stove, 26
Taj Mahal, 30
Tax burden, 96, 108
Tax court, 103

Tax deductible, 20, 95
Tax deduction, allowable, 28
Tax lien, 69
Tax specialist, 28
Tax strategy, 28
Taxes, 12, 13, 20, 61, 101, 107
Tenant(s), 5, 25, 26, 27, 28, 31, 63, 74, 85, 86, 87, 88, 89, 90, 91, 92, 93
Title company, 31, 41, 74, 76
Title insurance, 69
Title report, 69
Unassumable, 54
United States, 39
Utilities, 23
VA entitlement, 39, 40, 42, 43
VA foreclosure(s), 58, 64
VA loan, 9, 21, 31, 33, 42, 43
VAONLINE.VA.GOV, 40
VA-pamphlet 26-4, 40
VA-pamphlet 25-6, 40
Vacancy, 12, 22, 23, 24, 89
Vacancy factor, 23, 24
Variable interest rate loan, 32, 33
Verification of employment, 50
Veterans Administration (VA), 32, 35, 36, 39, 40, 41, 58, 59, 60, 61, 62, 63, 64, 70, 85
Water damage, 36
Water leak, 36
Welfare, 87
Wells Fargo, 49, 55, 56
Wrap, 74
Yellow pages, 26
WWW.VA.GOV, 40

To order additional copies of **An Intelligent Approach to Buying Real Estate,** complete the information below.

Ship to: (please print)

Name_____

Address_____

City, State, Zip _____

Day Phone_____

_____ copies of **An Intelligent Approach**
To Buying Real Estate @ $24.95 each $_____
Postage and handling @ $2.50 per book $_____
California residents add 8.25% sales tax
($2.06 per book) $_____
Total Enclosed $_____

Method of payment: ☐ Check   ☐ Credit Card: ☐ MC   ☐ VISA

Number _____ Exp. Date _____

Card user's
signature:_____

Make checks payable to **Cave Publishing**

Mail your order to: Cave Publishing
P.O.Box 282, Newbury Park, CA 91319

For you convenience, credit card customers call:
1-800-341-0914